¢OMMON $ENSE

THINGS *EVERYONE* SHOULD
KNOW ABOUT MONEY

BY MARK AMEERALI, B.COM

I would like to thank God, who has blessed my life immensely. Through Him alone this book is possible.

I would like to thank my parents, who showed me what hard work and perseverance can achieve.

I thank my loving and understanding wife, Jacqueline.

I am grateful to my family, my friends, and my colleagues, for helping to contribute to who I am today.

Cataloguing data available from Library and Archives Canada.

Published by the author.

Printed in Canada.

Acknowledgments

To those who helped me in the development of this book, particularly: Karl, Olga, Biddy, Jen, Nicole, Lee, Brett, Quinton, Brandon, Kwame, Layna, Derek, Karin, Davy, and Nancy.

Thank you.

Contents

Canada CUSTOMS 🇨🇦

LEVEL 3

The Little Book of Common Sense Investing

READ ☐

Canada CUSTOMS 🇨🇦

LEVEL 3

The Big Secret for the Small Investor

READ ☐

Canada CUSTOMS 🇨🇦

LEVEL 1

Ten Bad Habits We Learn In School

READ ☐

Achieving Passive Income

☐

Canada CUSTOMS 🇨🇦

Canada CUSTOMS 🇨🇦

LEVEL 1

Rich Dad's Cashflow Quadrant

READ ☐

Investing in ETFs

☐

Canada CUSTOMS 🇨🇦

Made a Budget!

☐

Canada CUSTOMS 🇨🇦

Canada CUSTOMS 🇨🇦

LEVEL 2

The Cottage, the Spider Brooch, & the Second Wife: How to Overcome the Challenges of Estate Planning

READ ☐

Canada CUSTOMS 🇨🇦

LEVEL 3

Index Funds: The 12-Step Recovery Program for Active Investors

READ ☐

Canada CUSTOMS 🇨🇦

LEVEL 1

The 10 Secrets Revenue Canada Doesn't Want You to Know

READ ☐

Canada CUSTOMS

LEVEL 2

Rich Dad's Guide to Investing

READ ☐

Investing in Real Estate

☐

Canada CUSTOMS 🇨🇦

Canada CUSTOMS 🍁
LEVEL 1
The Wealthy Barber
READ ☐

Canada CUSTOMS 🍁
LEVEL 1
7 Habits of Highly Effective People
READ ☐

Canada CUSTOMS 🍁
LEVEL 1
How to Rob Your Bank
READ ☐

FINANCIAL FREEDOM
☐
Canada CUSTOMS 🍁

Canada CUSTOMS 🍁
LEVEL 1
Rich Dad Poor Dad
READ ☐

Canada CUSTOMS 🍁
LEVEL 2
Unfair Advantage: The Power Of Financial Education
READ ☐

Investing in Exempt Markets
☐
Canada CUSTOMS 🍁

Canada CUSTOMS 🍁
LEVEL 1
How to Win Friends and Influence People
READ ☐

Canada CUSTOMS 🍁
LEVEL 1
The Wealthy Barber Returns
READ ☐

Canada CUSTOMS 🍁
LEVEL 3
The Empowered Investor
READ ☐

Canada CUSTOMS
LEVEL 3
Simple Wealth, Inevitable Wealth
READ ☐

Canada CUSTOMS 🍁
LEVEL 1
Personal Finance For Canadians For Dummies
READ ☐

Started Saving
☐
Canada CUSTOMS 🍁

Canada CUSTOMS 🍁
LEVEL 2
What the Average Joe Needs to Know
READ ☐

PREFACE

My story starts in a ghetto in the Caribbean country of Trinidad and Tobago. A little girl just seven years old was cast out of her home and left to survive on her own. It didn't take long for her to figure out that she couldn't make it alone. She was eventually taken in by nuns who ran a local convent. She was cared for, fed, clothed, and raised until the age of 18.

The girl showed exceptional talent in academics and a gift for sharing her knowledge with her peers. It wasn't long before the nuns recognized that she was a gifted child, who deserved a chance at a better life than they could afford to provide for her. Strings were pulled and many favors called in; as a result, the young woman found herself as a college student in New Westminster, Canada. She fell in love, married, and started a family before she was able to finish her degree in education. Five children were born to this family; I was the second child.

My parents were new immigrants, lacking both education and experience. They struggled to support five children, with my mother's insistence that her children attend private Catholic schools adding to the financial strain. My father got a job cleaning hospital floors shortly before I was born. He would return to school full-time, while working night shifts at the hospital. My mother cleaned houses and delivered newspapers at 4:00 A.M. each morning. One of the benefits of having so many children was she had a few helpers on those cold and often wet Vancouver mornings.

One morning in particular, my mother was sick, and my father was delivering newspapers when our furnace caught fire. Luckily, on a rare 2:00 A.M. bathroom trip, I just happened to smell the smoke. Our family escaped, but we lost almost everything in the fire.

A year later, my aunt died of a brain hemorrhage, leaving her three youngest children to fend for themselves on the streets of Trinidad. After going through a difficult adoption process, my parents now had eight children, and I had three new siblings. While this was a beautiful thing for my parents to do, it didn't necessarily help the family's financial situation.

My father eventually finished his degree when I was 12. He started teaching by day while maintaining his job at the hospital by night. My mother went to school, and it was no surprise to anyone that she was top of her class. She finished her degree when I was 16. By the time she returned to school, on a scholarship to complete her masters, we were attending the same campus. At this writing, my mom is the principal of a high school in Alberta, Canada. My father currently works one job and has time to dabble in any business venture he chooses.

I have an idea of what it's like to grow up in the wrong parts of town, to go without the luxuries or the comforts your friends have. I know what it's like to not have the right clothes, or the right skin colour, or the right background. I can tell you, none of that matters as much as your desire to succeed in life. My parents taught me that.

My parents are living examples of what it means to pursue your dreams. They certainly had their challenges, but after a 30 year struggle, achieved for themselves what they set out to find in Canada: a better life. They found their better life, and they were able to provide their children with more opportunities than they had.

I was fortunate to attend decent schools and a good university. Despite the fact that I was never the top student in any academic class, I always hovered near the top. Whenever I did struggle, I had the benefit of a fantastic tutor. My mom made sure we kept on top of our studies and ingrained in me her amazing work ethic, to which I attribute many of my achievements.

I hope most people reading this will find themselves able to take action and advantage of almost everything contained in this book. I would encourage you to thank your parents, grandparents, and everyone who sacrificed to make sure that was the case. If you find yourself struggling, just remember that your best asset is your own desire to change your circumstances and demand more for yourself.

When I was younger, I would frequently reflect on the struggle my parents endured to provide me with opportunities they never had. I saw it as an obligation to be successful in whatever I pursued. Now that I have been able to achieve so many of my goals, I wish to help others do the same. I hope this book will encourage you to achieve your goals. Believe in yourself; one day you will get there.

INTRODUCTION

Imagine life in the 1950's; the world was much less financially complex. It's likely that all the average person needed to know, was how to work and save to retire. Investing was not really a concern. Unfortunately, the world is no longer that simple, and the education system has failed to keep up with the complexities of teaching students how to survive financially in this fast paced new world. It's tough to blame educators, many of them were never taught anything about money.

If not in school, where are we supposed to learn how to manage our finances? Besides general happiness and good health, people's wealth usually ranks as their next highest priority. If they are not presently sick, money is their primary daily concern.

Where are people supposed to learn about such extremely important subjects? Our schools, where so much of the world's learning occurs, largely ignore both health and wealth, among many more important issues. I have issues with the lack of real world knowledge students gain in high school. I believe the system does a poor job of teaching students how to function as a contributing member of society. The system leaves students to figure out for themselves important issues such as: health and nutrition, finances, politics, mechanics, law, world religion, environmental sustainability, human relationships, and many more. Even at university, students major in one or two of these subjects at the expense of the others. Why not make these important topics requirements for high school graduation? What do we have to lose, pre-calculus, or English? Honestly, what is more useful to the student? Learning how to draw pictures with trigonometry and write longer essays, or learning how to avoid a life time of debt and poor health? How many of the academic skills we learn in school translate into applicable real life tools?

When a student decides to enter higher education, they must choose a course of study, but more importantly, they must decide what they intend on doing after graduation. Schools should provide a map to undergraduates on their first day, describing the likely careers that develop from each major, including hiring statistics from their school and the matching incomes associated with each career path. The business school I attended did this, which I found phenomenally useful. This would aid in preventing so many university graduates from feeling let down by their schools and regarding their hard earned degree as useless. Too few university graduates find work in their chosen field of study. The severe mismatch between skills/education and outcome is shocking. You have to start wondering if the schools really know what the world looks like or if they even care. Are they simply selling education whether it is useful or not? Do they really care how useful their product is if people continue to buy it anyway? When you begin with the end in mind, it is much easier to get somewhere useful.

HOW TO USE THIS BOOK

Despite spending the majority of my career in the financial world, I am not a big fan of mathematics and formulas. I am however, a very big fan of pictures and graphs. I have made every attempt to make this book as visually stimulating and interactive as possible. If a picture is worth a thousand words, I've saved a few trees by including so many images in this book. Of course, it's still a book, but it is packed with visuals, book recommendations, and links to other resources such as videos and websites. As a student of learning, I am aware that reading is the least effective way to learn. That's why there are so many opportunities to link to online tools.

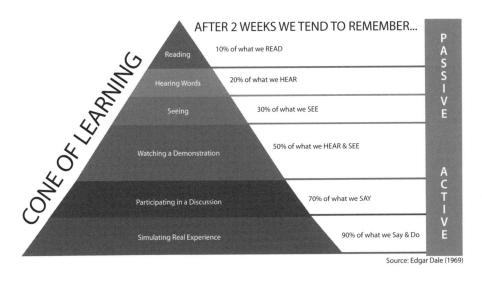

AFTER 2 WEEKS WE TEND TO REMEMBER...

CONE OF LEARNING

Reading	10% of what we READ	PASSIVE
Hearing Words	20% of what we HEAR	
Seeing	30% of what we SEE	
Watching a Demonstration	50% of what we HEAR & SEE	
Participating in a Discussion	70% of what we SAY	ACTIVE
Simulating Real Experience	90% of what we Say & Do	

Source: Edgar Dale (1969)

I want you to think of this book as a passport, instead of an encyclopedia. I will recommend useful resources which expand on the subjects we will cover. Each supplementary resource you can access to compliment this cornerstone book will deepen your understanding, increasing your likelihood of success.

If this book is a passport, my website is an airport. All of the recommended resources can be accessed from: **www.mymoneysense.ca**. There you will find your boarding passes to all of the amazon book links, web tool links, and links to videos. There is a lot of bonus material on the site, not mentioned in the book. You can also contact me through the site.

Also available on the website is a gateway to the free education portal. Here, you can access teaching material such as videos, slide decks, tests, answers, articles I'm reading, and even my personal blog. There is also a Q&A forum. In the future, I hope to create both a social and solo game to allow people to learn in a fun way. I want to eventually host a national financial challenge; it will allow students the opportunity to write a test and receive scholarships and internship interviews for their achievements and allow employers the opportunity to observe student progress.

Some of the books I recommend are written on a basic level, giving a broader understanding of the subject. Other books delve more deeply into particular topics. You will find this leveling system useful to help you decide which books to read and in what order.

Level 1: Written on a high school level
Level 2: Written on a college level
Level 3: Written on a university level

There is a visa page at the front to mark off the books you have read. It also includes landmarks on your path to financial freedom. If you take the time to read all of these books, you will be well on your way to success.

I have also developed a system of icons that will help to alert you to important content throughout the book:

Glossary terms are in **bold**. Web resources are *italicized* and are all accessible through **www.mymoneysense.ca.** You are encouraged to visit all links immediately for maximum effectiveness.

WHY I WROTE THIS BOOK

You don't need to be an expert to learn the basics of complex ideas. This book is designed to get you started on the path. A complete discussion of every idea in this book would result in a volume of biblical proportions (excuse the pun).

I want to assure the reader of my motivation for writing this book and explain the tone in which it is written. I'm driven by the desire to try to leave the world a better place. This is the essential information I want to pass on to my children in the areas of personal finance and investments, with a sprinkling of general wisdom, but it is useful for everyone. The profits from this book and the enterprise tied to it, are dedicated to increasing the level of financial literacy in Canadian youth.

Keep in mind that all the money and freedom in the world will be useless without your health. So please, take care of your body, it has to last you a lifetime. After that, consider how you want to spend your time, where you want to spend your time, and with whom. Time, not money is the most precious resource you have. Spend it wisely.

As an individual, there is only so much that I can do to help any charity or aid group. However, if I can free a large chunk of time and money for the next generation, the impact on the world increases many-fold. I hope this book will go a long way in helping many people to become financially free and able to use their time to do good for others. I find it's much easier to help make a better world when you are on solid financial ground. So please, when you find yourself stable and able, consider helping out those less fortunate in any way you see fit.

When it comes to achieving financial freedom, never underestimate the importance of time and starting early. The time is now; you have your whole future ahead of you. The sooner you start to apply the principles in this book, the easier it will be for you to achieve your financial freedom. So, you better get started.

On the topic, getting started, I have a foundational book recommendation. This book will help you to proactively engage in life and achieve your goals.

Stephen R. Covey. *7 Habits of Highly Effective People.*

From a very young age, I focused on one single financial goal: to achieve financial freedom. My definition of financial freedom is having **passive income** larger than my expenses. Passive income is income that you don't have to actively work to earn. There are many different ways you can achieve this. Focusing on earning passive income through real estate and helping others to do the same is a personal goal of mine. Many people choose to own small businesses, while others benefit from royalties or licences. Whichever path you choose, make sure to buy assets that put money in your pocket.

Your ideal life begins at true financial freedom. The habits you set early in your life will persist; you decide through today's actions who you will be in the future. I hope you will bring honor and respect to those who meet you on your path to financial freedom and your ideal life.

Expenses ❮ Passive Income ═ *Financial Freedom*

This is the key to your financial freedom; always remember this equation.

I believe that when you release a person from the stress of having to support themselves and their family, it is easier for them to be who they truly want to be. They can choose to be more generous, more caring, more loving, and more compassionate. I hope you will find some wisdom in this book that will help you to be the best possible version of yourself. Here's to finding your financial freedom.

If you have ever heard someone say: "If I knew then, what I know now...", consider this your "then", and take advantage.

Chapter 0
Don't Just Do What Everyone Else Does

"Dig deep down and ask yourself, who do you want to be? ... I'm talking about figuring out for yourselves what makes you happy. You have to think outside the box, that's what I believe. After all, what is the point of being on this earth if all you want to do is be liked by everyone and avoid trouble?"
- Arnold Schwarzenegger

In this chapter, I will summarize many other books in personal finance and investing. The ideas detailed in these books were fantastic for the time they were written; people need something new and relevant for their time. These books provided the reader with some very essential information, but in current times they often fall short, because they outline an overly simplified plan for investing, without providing a second step. There is no road map to know where to get the next piece of vital information. It is not enough to provide the reader with only enough information to find themselves at the beginning of the pipeline of regular retail financial services. People want to truly understand why they should use financial services, and more importantly, they deserve to have the tools to properly assess which services are best for them.

Retail financial services are the kind of services you will easily see marketed at the bank, on the street, on TV, or in magazines and newspapers. Most people feel that this is a good starting point if they don't know a thing about investing. I'm not saying these people are wrong, but if people knew what they were doing, their choices would change dramatically. As you can probably imagine, the most widely available and easily accessible investment options may not be the best. Someone using standard retail investments such as actively managed mutual funds, has not found their financial freedom but simply reached the next level of financial slavery.

Let's begin by summarizing many of the essential elements of a typical beginner's investment book. I will highlight some of the key things a savvy investor would take advantage of, pointing out areas where more knowledge could mean big savings and large increases in results. I'm talking about simple decisions made differently that can save you and possibly make you, hundreds of thousands of dollars.

Typical beginner's investment books often overlook many important topics for the sake of simplicity. For example, they neglect to explain how your money is taxed. They don't tell you how the advisors or authors invest their own money. They don't teach you about options which exist outside the stock market or products the authors sell. I can understand that they don't want to overcomplicate their book, discouraging and overwhelming the reader. However, without at least an elementary understanding of what options are available outside mainstream investments, an investor turns a blind eye to them altogether. This is advantageous primarily to financial service representatives who want to 'help' you invest your money.

I want to be clear that I do not believe that those who work in financial services are bad people. In many cases, they honestly want to do what is in the best interest of their clients. The problem is, the bottom tier of investment professionals usually have the least amount of access to the best opportunities, and they are only compensated for what they can sell. Therefore, they are not motivated to learn about all the things clients can buy outside of their products. The only way to climb that ladder of opportunity is to learn that there is a higher rung and reach for it. This book provides that higher rung, and guess what? You need to reach to get there. I am going to challenge the way you think about money, time, and opportunity. So, let's get started.

A BRIEF SUMMARY OF A TYPICAL BEGINNER'S INVESTMENT BOOK:

Start now
Pay yourself first
Create a budget
Follow an investment plan
Save for a rainy day

These are all excellent points, which I will review briefly in this chapter. I will expand on some of these later in the book, as well as extend this list:

- **Learn about taxes and how to keep more of your money**
- **Learn about mortgages and how to save yourself thousands**
- **Learn about stocks and how they work**
- **Learn about mutual funds and why you may not want to use them**
- **Learn about bonds and how they work**
- **Learn about economics and why it's so important to your life**
- **Learn about pensions and insurance and how important they are**
- **Learn about what makes a typical investment plan**
- **Learn about alternatives to the typical investment plan**
- **Learn how to create an investment plan for yourself**

As I mentioned before, I do not intend to go into the details of every alternative or every investment option. Using this book as a cornerstone of knowledge will allow you to build a strong foundation for your financial future. The books I recommend on the visa page allow you to start building on that foundation. When you make it through this book and all the recommended books, you will know more about investing and financial planning than 95% of the people on the planet. You will also have probably read more on the subject than most entry level financial planners and be better equipped to invest your money than they are.

Here is the standard investment book condensed into one chapter.

START NOW

People want you to invest today, because your money today is worth so much more than your money in the future. The reason being, as you invest your money grows. The longer the time period (or investment horizon, in technical terms), the more potential your money has to multiply. I will talk about this in considerable detail, because understanding this is the most essential and basic lesson for any investor. Time is money.

PAY YOURSELF FIRST

Forced saving plans are necessary for most people. If it were easy not to spend too much money and have some left to invest at the end of the month, credit card debt would be rare. It is not. I can honestly say, I am a normal person. There is absolutely no shame in being normal. The way to get abnormal results is to plan, educate, and discipline yourself. I'm a big fan of doing the most difficult things first, because you know things are always going to get easier. I'm telling you now, the most difficult thing about investing is finding the money to start. The easiest way to do this is to force yourself to do it by making sure it's the first thing you do. I recommend David Chilton's 10% strategy here (found in *The Wealthy Barber*). If you set up an automatic 10% direct deposit to an investment account, you won't even miss the money. In younger years, you may even be able to save up to 50%, which will make a huge difference to your retirement plan.

In chapters 3 and 5, I will explain how much money your current savings can be worth compared to your future savings. You are going to wish that you started saving the day you started earning. If you haven't started earning yet, congratulations. This book was written with you in mind.

CREATE A BUDGET

It's self-evident that paying yourself first will mean nothing if you have to continuously dip into savings to compensate for your over spending on a monthly basis. Discipline and having a plan will help you. I'm not going to waste space by telling you not to overspend. However, what I will do is challenge you to think clearly about your budget. If you are not able to afford what you want, put some thought into how you can expand your income to be able to afford it, instead of simply cutting it out.

Robert Kiyosaki made this an important theme of his best selling book, *Rich Dad Poor Dad*. He suggests expanding your means or your income and asking "How can I afford this?" instead of always saying "I can't afford this." Robert also developed Cashflow®, a fun and interactive game to teach important financial lessons. I love this game and play regularly with my students.

Rich Dad Poor Dad was one of the first books I ever read and was influential in how I thought about money. Not wanting to live within a constrictive budget, I applied the "expansion of means" idea. Adopting this principle to expand my income, I designed my first course in financial literacy when I was a summer intern with a wealth management firm in Vancouver. I was about to enter my last year of university, and I didn't have a lot of savings, nor did I make much money, but I wanted to be able to park my car downtown with the big brokers. I taught my course at the university's "mini school", a fun learning program where students can take non-credit classes in subjects of interest to them. The extra income from teaching this course paid for my parking and lunches downtown and showed me that I loved teaching others about finance. Years later, I'm writing this book as a direct result of that experience.

FOLLOW AN INVESTMENT PLAN

I'm not into wasting words, time, or effort. The majority of this book is designed to educate the reader about the elements that make an investment plan and guide them towards the ability to create one for themselves. It won't matter if you have the best plan out there, if you don't fund or follow it. I recommend saving 10% immediately, via a direct deposit into your investment account. You will quickly realize that you don't even miss the money.

Chapter 11 assimilates many of the ideas in the book into a few different examples of investment plans. These are for your reference only. However, you may find the explanations of the different plans useful when formulating your own.

SAVE FOR A RAINY DAY

In today's ever changing employment environment, you could find yourself out on your butt and unemployed in a heartbeat. Most employers will discard you the moment you become inconvenient. If you have any doubts about this, ask people who have been working for a while and you will learn pretty fast that what I'm saying is true. I know this from personal experience. Furthermore, sickness, disaster, and any number of things can threaten your financial security.

It is your responsibility to make sure that what should be a financial flesh wound is not a kill shot. In order to make sure you're not on the ropes the first time life deals you a punch to the nose, you need to prepare like it will eventually happen one day. If you are prepared for the unexpected, with proper insurance and an emergency fund, the worst thing that will happen to you is that you never have to use it. Let's hope that's the case.

An easy way to create an emergency fund is to take out a line of credit BEFORE you need it and while you have a steady income. You won't owe interest on the funds if you don't use them, and the bank can't take it back if you lose your job. You can also use it to pay itself if you absolutely have to (more on this later).

 I don't think it's a waste time to get a second opinion, especially when it comes to your health or your wealth. If you feel like reading a starter book just to see what others are saying, I have a popular one to recommend which I enjoyed immensely. It's called:

The Wealthy Barber, by David Chilton, and it is a very well written book for its time. If you are going to read Chilton's first book, I highly recommend the sequel: *The Wealthy Barber Returns*. Written two decades later, there are some very important contrasts between the first and second book.

SUMMARY

At this point, you may be thinking, "I have to save, make a budget, and get some investments." You would be right, and you would probably head to your local bank or investment company to start looking for help. Well, this is not your average beginner's book, and in the 21st century, you are going to have to do a lot more for a passing grade.

Chapter 1
Taxes: You're Richer Than You Think

"I'm in favor of cutting taxes under any circumstances, and for any excuse, for any reason, whenever it's possible." - Milton Friedman

You are going to pay taxes all your life, so it's important for you to understand the basics of the taxation system, more specifically, income taxes in a progressive tax system. I honestly can't believe that this subject is not taught in 9th grade before most people get their first job. However, it's largely ignored, and you can do something to remedy that. If you are in high school and have an interest in some self directed learning, I encourage you to research a financial literacy program called: "The City," provided by the Government of Canada and the BC Securities Commission. It is found on the Government of Canada's website in the *Financial Consumer Agency education section.*[1]

I know that taxes are not an exciting subject for most people, but that doesn't diminish its importance. The average Canadian will lose almost a quarter of their money to income taxes before they even get their hands on it. Considering all taxes (sales, liquor, property, fuel, etc), Canadians lose close to half their money to taxes. If there is one thing you should understand about money, it should be how to keep more of what you have earned.

HOW TO CALCULATE YOUR TAXES

Many people could use a little help in understanding the way their income is taxed. First, you probably have a different tax situation than your neighbor, so it's important to get professional advice. You are being taxed based on a marginal tax system. This means, the higher your income level, the more taxes you are 'supposed' to pay.

Often times, people confuse 'gross' and 'net' income. Think of your income dollars like little fish in the ocean. Everything you catch in your 'net' you keep, and every time you think about how much you could have captured, you feel gross. So, your net income is what you keep.

In general, a progressive tax system is a more complicated version of this:

SIMPLIFIED TAX SYSTEM

Tax Level

$100,000	40 %
$75,000	30 %
$40,000	20 %
$10,000	0 %

LEVEL 1: NO TAX

At the first level of our imaginary progressive marginal tax system, there is no income tax. The logic behind this is, if you are only earning less than $10,000, you don't make enough money for the government to justify taxing what little you have earned.

In our simplified example, we assume the first level or "tax bracket" is $0 - $10,000.

LEVEL 2: AT THIS LEVEL YOU START PAYING TAX

This will be where you pay the lowest percentage of tax. It's important to note that you only pay the tax rate for the money that is in that tax bracket. In our example, the tax rate in level 2 is 20%. You would only pay 20% tax on the dollars between $10,000 and $40,000. So, $30,000 x 20% = $6,000 owing in tax.

LEVEL 3: CONTINUING UP THE LADDER

The tax rate increases with your income. In our simplified example, for every dollar you earn between $40,000 and $75,000, you pay 30% in tax.

LEVEL 4: THE HIGHEST LEVEL

In our example, for every dollar you earn above $75,000, you pay 40% in tax. To add up your total taxes owing, if you earned $100,000 in common sense land, you would calculate all the income tax you owed using this simple method.

Below $10,000 = $0
$10,000 - $40,000: $30,000 x 20% = $6,000
$40,000 - $75,000: $35,000 x 30% = $10,500
$75,000 - $100,000: $25,000 x 40% = $10,000
Total tax owed = $26,500 for an average tax rate of 26.5%.

Unfortunately, income tax is not the only deduction coming off your paycheck. Government pension plans and employment insurance will also show up. Rather, they will appear on your pay stub to tell you why more money is <u>not</u> showing up. At the end of the year, you receive what is called a T4 slip from your employer. When you file your yearly taxes, this piece of paper is essential to ensure you submit the correct numbers. For many employed people, paying taxes is a simple exercise of taking information from their T4, and ensuring their employer has deducted the correct amount of tax from each paycheck throughout the year. If this is the case, the government acknowledges this and no additional tax is owed. If for some reason your employer took too little or too much tax, or if you find you are eligible for extra deductions, you may owe more tax or get a tax refund. Visit the LSM Insurance website to try out an *income tax calculator.*[2]

Keep in mind, you may qualify for additional deductions due to your personal tax situation. I recommend having a tax professional review your situation. Alternatively, you could purchase tax software to help you. I have heard great reviews about *TurboTax.*[3]

TAXES FOR BUSINESS

The previous example calculated the taxes for an employee making $100,000 per year. Let's imagine that person wasn't an employee, but a small business owner. How would their taxes change their net income?

 In general, an employee follows this process: work, get taxed, get paid, and spend money. For a business owner, there is a very important change: work (maybe), spend money, get paid, and get taxed. Did you notice that the business owner gets to spend money before they get taxed? This may not seem like a big deal, but it is a very big deal. This means that the business owner is taxed after they spend money on business expenses.

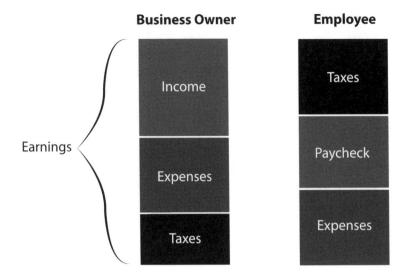

This opens a very important discussion about the beautiful world of tax deductions. A tax deduction or "write off" is a **bona fide** business expense, that a business owner is allowed to use to reduce their declared net income, before they pay tax on that income. This means that at the end of the year, the income left to be taxed is generally smaller than an employee making the same income. <u>At the end of the year, the business owner will pay less tax than an employee earning the same amount of income.</u> The other interesting thing to note is that the deductions for a business owner can get pretty liberal. Here are a few items you may never have thought that you could partially or fully "write off."

Phones, phone bills, cars/leases, gas, rent, meals, entertainment, car rental, flights, computers, software, stationary, internet bills, etc.

I'm certain that most people will be spending money on the items above. The question I have is, "Would you rather pay for them with pre-tax money, or with what's left? The tax deduction issue is the number one reason I recommend every person run some sort of business, no matter how small. It transforms you from a pure employee, who is fully taxed to the max, to an employee that has a business.

In our example of personal taxes, the employee making $100,000 was taxed $26,500 per year. Let's suppose a business owner with $100,000 in revenue, was able to write off $40,000 in expenses. This would leave $60,000 in taxable income remaining at the end of the year. Remember, the business gets to pay taxes after the year ends, essentially getting an interest free loan from the government. In our simplified tax schedule, the business owner would owe only $12,000 in tax. That's 55% less tax, a $14,500 tax discount!

When you have a business, you get tax deductions; plain and simple, even if your business is a home based multi-level marketing operation. You know the ones that people continuously assume are illegal pyramid schemes? People in direct sales know tax deductions very well. These people almost always have a primary job but have chosen to try to add to their income by starting a small business in their own name. Because they have started a business, they are able to access many of the wonderful tax deductions that any business gets. When you start a business in your own name, you are a **sole proprietor**. This means that you get to access the tax deductions in your own name, against your own employment income as well as your business income.

There are many other ways to go about starting a business. This is a very complex area, and whole books are written on this alone. In fact, many books are written on this, and I can recommend a couple of easy reads. For now, just realize that as a pure employee, you are likely to be paying more tax than anyone else because you have the fewest tax "breaks" and deductions.

Check out *taxbot*[4] to help you keep track of your deductions if you run a small business.

 Robert Kiyosaki has written another wonderful book called *Cashflow Quadrant* on the subject of the different kinds of taxes for different types of people: employees, self-employed people, business owners, and investors. I encourage you to read this book to discover which path makes most sense for you. I can honestly say that reading this book was instrumental in pushing me towards business ownership.

 For my fellow Canadian readers, there is a fantastic book called *The 10 Secrets Canada Revenue Doesn't Want You to Know* by David M. Voth.[5] This book creates the correct kind of awareness regarding hanging on to your hard earned money.

TAXES FOR INVESTORS

If you've ever had a conversation about saving money for retirement, you have probably come across the idea of a tax deferred retirement plan. This is a vehicle, or special account that allows you to invest money without paying any tax until the end stage of the plan. If you live in Canada, this is called your RRSP, which means Registered Retirement Savings Plan. More recently, the Canadian government has added a new special type of account called a TFSA, meaning Tax Free Savings Account.

It's important to understand the benefits of each of these accounts. Let's summarize the basic highlight for each one; with the RRSP, you get an up-front tax credit for depositing money into this account, but are taxed when you take money out. With the TFSA, you don't get a tax credit for contributing, but you're not taxed on any gains inside the account; you can withdraw money, tax free. Both of the accounts have limits on how much you can contribute in a single year. You can learn about both types of accounts on the *CRA (Canada Revenue Agency) website.*[6]

There are a lot of fantastic things to say about tax deferred plans. First, your gains from investment will not be taxed until the end of the plan. Another great attribute about RRSPs is that it's a tax deduction everyone gets to make; you can contribute to your RRSP with pre-tax dollars and have less taxable income at the end of the year. This will result in a lower amount of tax you have to pay to the government.

No RRSP Contribution

Gross Income

Tax

Net Income

RRSP Contribution

RRSP

Tax

Net Income

Here is the downside of the RRSP and something most investment books don't mention. While you do get a nice tax deduction or write-off for putting the money in your retirement plan, you are limited to only "government approved" investments with the money in your retirement account. Some of the best investment opportunities are outside that government approved list of investments. Be aware that the government approved list focuses on the world of publicly listed securities and mutual funds. However, **ETFs (Exchange-Traded Funds)**, index funds, and many exempt market investments are also on this list; I will have a lot to say about those later.

It's also worth mentioning that many successful people find themselves in a higher tax bracket in retirement than in their working years. This is a downer for those who have saved and invested well and find themselves paying more tax than ever when they withdraw money.

Chapter 2
As Safe As Money In The Bank

"It is well enough that people of the nation do not understand our banking and monetary system, for if they did, I believe there would be a revolution before tomorrow morning." - Henry Ford

I have worked for three of Canada's chartered banks, in retail, commercial, and wealth management. My reasons for leaving the banks centre around the fact that there is a vast problem surrounding information sharing. This means that one person has a lot of information that the other person does not. This can create some ethical problems if you are advising people about what to do with their money.

There is a lot of information that could help you out when dealing with the banks, that they will not give you freely. First, let's look at why the bank exists. The bank's main function is to be a financial intermediary, meaning they match the users of funds (the borrowers) to the savers of funds (the lenders). But the banks don't stop at lending out other people's money, they lend it over and over again, more than 10 times the original deposit amount!

The goal of the bank is the same as all other corporations in the world: to maximize shareholder profit. When you observe big companies acting irresponsibly, remember the primary goal of a corporation is to maximize shareholder wealth. The shareholders are faceless and nameless to the client; they bear no responsibility for the actions of the corporation.

I'm not suggesting that the teller at your bank is an evil person executing some evil plan to steal your money and ruin the world with it. The tellers, those smiling people who help to execute your transactions, are blameless in the grand scheme of things. However, as one goes further up the ladder, those ethical lines that were so clear on the ground floor become blurred.

The key employees of the banking corporation are compensated by the amount of money they make for the shareholders. As long as they act within the law, they can go home happy. There is a large gap between what is legal and what is ethical; do not ever forget this. Many times in your life you will be asked to compromise what is right for what is legal. These choices will define you, so choose wisely.

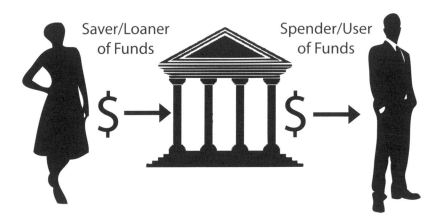

The banks are not the only financial intermediary that exist. Credit unions also act as the connection between those who need money and those who have extra. Credit unions are not for profit organizations. The money they make is poured back into the communities in which they are based. A credit union answers to its members, not to a board of directors representing anonymous shareholders. Credit unions are not as ubiquitous as banks, but they are growing in number, size, and influence. I would encourage you to analyze the difference between banks and credit unions, and choose your institution wisely. Your decision will have an impact on your money and finances, as well as an impact on the distribution of wealth in the economy and your own community. I will give an example of this idea in chapter 8, when I describe two towns: Edgewater and Bridgewater.

BANK ACCOUNTS

When deciding where you want to hold your money, consider that some banking institutions (most banks) will charge you a monthly fee just to hold your money for you. When they make money by lending your money out, you may start to wonder why they are charging you to hold your money, considering that lending out your money is a profit maker for them. Often, banks will also charge you to access your money, via withdrawal or transaction fees. If you see a problem with this system, consider voicing your concern by selecting your financial institution wisely.

CREDIT CARDS

"Remember that credit is money." - Ben Franklin

This is one section that parents will be thanking me for writing. The number one rule with credit cards is: DO NOT carry a balance. Pay off your credit card every month, and refrain from spending money you don't have. A credit card is completely different to a debit card.

People tend to overspend when they are using their credit card instead of their debit card. Women shopping in pairs or groups will usually overspend the most.

The key here is self control. You can maintain control of your spending for 29 days of the month and slip on just a single day. That won't erase the fact that you slipped, and the debt will remain regardless. I'm not saying never spend; I'm saying, control your spending. If you are having trouble with this, try leaving your cards at home and carrying cash or waiting a week before making pleasure purchases.

To drive this point home, I suggest watching an interesting TED talk by

Joachim de Posada, called: *Don't Eat the Marshmallow.*[7] If you don't know about TED talks, I strongly recommend you visit *ted.com*[8], and replace anytime you waste on YouTube with this. The talk was based on a study of immediate versus delayed gratification and its long-term results on success.

American children, about four years old, were left alone in a classroom. A psychology professor placed a marshmallow on their desk, explaining that if they resisted the temptation to eat the marshmallow for 15 minutes they would get two marshmallows. Over 600 children participated in the experiment at different hours of the day.

Result: When the professor left the room, 66% of the children immediately ate the marshmallow. Here's where it gets interesting; 15 years later, these kids were tracked down. Of the 33% who didn't eat the marshmallow, all of them were successfully pursuing their goals; none were in jail, none had dropped out of school, and they all had good relationships with their teachers. Their SAT grades were 213 points higher on average than the kids who ate the marshmallow. Of the kids who ate the marshmallow, a large percentage were in trouble; only a few had good grades, some of them had dropped out, and a few were still in school but with bad grades.

Lesson: If you want to succeed, you have to learn to delay gratification. Nowhere is this more true than in the world of finance. Once you slip up, creating too much bad debt, you can bury yourself.

Here is an example of how expensive a credit card can be:

Buying a TV for $1,000, and making the minimum payments for 30 years at 21%.

Your minimum payment may be as low as $17.21. At first glance, this looks like an attractive offer for that TV you just have to have, but remember, delay delay delay that gratification, and reap the rewards. Let's look at how much financial pain that self control will save you.

If you were to make the minimum payments for the full 30 year amortization (repayment) period, your total payments would be $6,321.60. All but $1,000 of that would be interest. Essentially, you would be paying an extra $5,321.60 in interest. Your TV will not last as long as the payments.

Note that I arbitrarily chose a 30 year period. In fact, the credit card companies can make this repayment period over 100 years. They require just over 2% of the total payment per month. If you pay 2% back per month, but your interest rate is 22%, you will only be re-paying 2% of the principal balance per year (if you don't spend any more or incur additional fees!). This will make that TV very expensive. Look at your statement to find the repayment period.

When you find yourself trying to justify a purchase on your credit card, please remember this example. Think to yourself, "Instead of buying something that takes money out of my pocket, what can I buy that will make those payments for me?" This is how wealthy people train their children to think. After a while, it becomes second nature to buy an asset in order to finance a pleasure purchase.

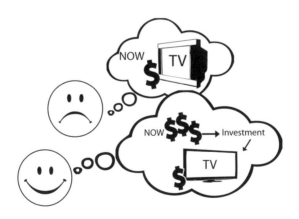

I know that what I have written above is the 'ideal' scenario. Sometimes, you have to carry a balance. In that case, let me help you out. The first thing I want to tell you about is a little secret the credit card companies will never advertise, but almost all offer. This is the Balance Of Account Transfer, or BOAT. A BOAT is when one credit card company pays another credit card company the debt you owe them. Why would they want to pay off your debt, you may ask? Well, the answer is easy, they would prefer to make some money rather than no money. So they are willing to transfer money to the other credit card for you and steal the business from the other company, often at rates less than 5%.

Example: Steve owes $10,000 to MasterCard for fixing up his Mustang with a cold air intake, a super charger, dual exhaust, and after market rims. He is loving what it does for him with the ladies, but he dies just a little inside when he sees his monthly credit card bill. At 21% annual interest, he owes a good chunk of his paycheck each month to MasterCard. Being a master at trying to get out of stuff, he calls the number on the back of his Visa card, and follows the prompts to speak to an agent to do a balance of account transfer. He successfully transfers the money to his Visa card, and while he still owes $10,000 for the same stupid reasons, he gets to pay it off for six months at just 4% interest instead of 21%. However, at the end of 6 months, it goes right back up to 21%. Can he BOAT the balance back to MasterCard, and flip it back to Visa again if he likes? I'm glad you asked, and the answer is yes.

 Read the fine print for your credit cards, and seek out at least one with a good BOAT rate, in case you need to use that feature. I usually have two credit cards, one that's good for rewards, and one that's good for BOATs. There are some fantastic rewards available out there: travel, merchandise, and rental car insurance. I love all that free stuff so I keep using my card. I spend only on the rewards card, and I transfer the balance to the low interest card only if I have to.

 Certain retailers and even gas stations offer special loyalty credit cards that earn you points. The cards often come with a gift or discount upon first use. They are credit cards in every sense of the word. The purchase rates often far exceed those on your normal credit card, sometimes as high as 29%! My advice to everyone would be to read the fine print and use it to your advantage.

Most credit cards have a grace period, which means that if you have a zero balance from the previous month, you are not immediately charged interest on new purchases. The grace period usually lasts until about three weeks after you receive your statement. This can be considered an interest free loan. Grace periods don't apply to cash advances (when you take money directly out of the bank machine with your credit card). Also, cash advances don't count toward rewards.

Try to avoid paying more than 20% interest on your credit cards by paying them off before the end of the grace period and using BOATs. Also, consider using a line of credit to pay off the credit card.

LINES OF CREDIT (LOC)

 A line of credit is like a special loan account that you can access with your bank card. It is different from both a bank account and a credit card. I personally think lines of credit are a very snazzy product, because they give you access to cheap (low rate), very accessible consumer credit. The purchase rate on a credit card is very high: around 10% - 28%, depending on where you got the card. A line of credit has much lower rates, usually less than half that of a credit card; yet you can take money out as if it were a bank account. The difference between a regular bank account and a line of credit (LOC) account is like the two sides of a thermometer. The LOC should never go above 0. Either you owe money or you don't, but you would never keep a positive balance. The other side is a bank account, where either you have money or you don't, but you usually wouldn't have a negative balance.

Also, the line of credit is "revolving" credit; it's not like a regular loan where you fill out an application, receive all the funds up front, and get charged interest right away. Instead, you apply once for a limit on the loan, and then you can access it when you like. While there is technically a repayment schedule, it is not as rigid as a typical loan. For example, if I have a $10,000 line of credit and I don't use it at all this month (I have a balance of 0), I pay no interest. If I draw out half the money, or $5,000, I will owe monthly interest on that money. I can start paying it back for the next few months, and if I want to take more out at any point, I can. In fact, I could "pay" my bill for this month and decide to take that money back out 10 seconds later if I wanted to. This is unlike a normal loan, where once you submit the loan payment, you can't get it back out.

 Lines of credit can be designed as unsecured. If you default on the loan (neglect to pay it) and go **bankrupt**, the lending institution will have no recourse. They can't take anything away from you to get their money back. However, you will badly damage your credit if you don't pay your bills (more on that later). With a typical secured loan, a car loan or house loan, if you stop paying, the lender takes that asset back.

Lines of credit are great; you get a lower rate than a credit card on an unsecured loan that is easy to access. I'm a big fan of LOCs, and I use mine regularly, not because I just like to borrow money and owe interest. Whenever I borrow money, it serves an important purpose (more on that later). Having a LOC also has the added benefit of developing my credit score.

CREDIT SCORES

Credit scores and their effect on your financial future are one of the most important subjects in this book. I know that they're not exciting, and I will be as succinct as possible. But, don't overlook this topic; it is one area where you can easily save yourself six figures as I will explain shortly. The Canada Revenue Agency tells us that, your credit score is a judgment about your financial health at a specific point in time. It indicates the risk you represent for lenders compared to other consumers.

There are a couple of different ways to work out credit scores. The credit-reporting agencies, Equifax and TransUnion, use a scale from 300 to 900. High scores on this scale are good; the higher your score, the lower the risk for the lender. Lenders may also have their own ways of arriving at credit scores. In addition, lenders must decide on the lowest score you can have and still borrow money from them. They can also use your score to set the interest rate you will pay.

WHAT DETERMINES YOUR CREDIT SCORE?

Each credit rating system is slightly different, but you can use this as a general guideline.

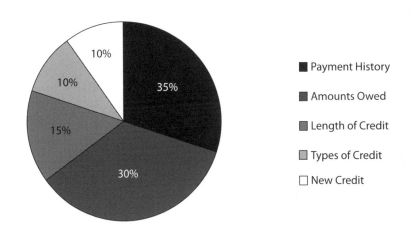

PAYMENT HISTORY

This is the most heavily weighted component of your credit score. If you don't have a history of paying your bills on time, it's going to show up as a big black mark on your credit history. Generally, a serious missed payment will remain on your report for 7 years.

AMOUNTS OWED

How much money you currently owe or have historically owed, plays a major factor in your credit score. If someone has $10,000 in available credit, and generally owes $9,000, it is not going to reflect kindly on their credit score. Just one nudge in the wrong direction and that person could easily find themselves bankrupt. I recommend never carrying a balance over 50% of your consumer credit capacity if you can avoid it.

Consumer credit: a debt that someone incurs for the purpose of purchasing a good or service. This includes purchases made on credit cards, lines of credit, and some loans.

LENGTH OF CREDIT HISTORY

If you are young, or new to the country, and are trying to establish your credit for the first time, you will not have a high credit score; you have no history of payments to prove your credit worthiness.

TYPES OF CREDIT USED

Using different types of credit benefits your credit score. You can easily prove yourself trustworthy with a couple of credit cards and a line of credit. The responsible use of revolving credit develops more credit history and boosts your score.

NEW CREDIT

When you get a new credit card or a new loan, it is an opportunity for you to prove yourself worthy. In the short term however, it means that you are further able to damage your reputation with a lender if you decide to neglect your responsibility. Your credit score may dip after you get a new credit tool until you prove that you can service the new debt responsibly.

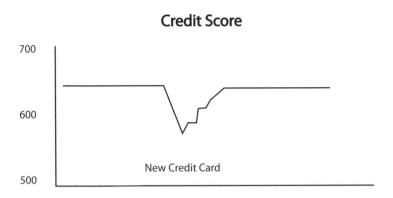

WHERE CAN I GET MY CREDIT SCORE?

Along with the credit histories of millions of other people, your credit history is recorded in files maintained by at least one of the major credit-reporting agencies: *Equifax Canada*[9] and *TransUnion Canada.*[10] It is possible to obtain your credit file for free. Please consult the agencies' websites in order to obtain more information. These files are called credit reports; a credit report is a snapshot of your credit history. It is one of the main tools lenders use to decide whether or not to give you credit.

HOW CAN I RAISE MY CREDIT SCORE?

First, and most importantly, never miss a payment. With the abundance of products and providers in today's market, sometimes things can slip. I recommend using *mint*[11] or a similar service to help keep you organized. Frequent use of credit products shows creditors that you are a responsible user of credit. Keeping your credit use ratios within acceptable levels means that your card isn't sitting at 90% capacity at all times. Try not to let your balance remain over 50% of the total allowable amount.

Having multiple credit products (one line of credit and two credit cards) and using them frequently can raise your credit score. Paying a monthly bill like a cell phone will not raise your credit score. It will only damage your score if the bill is sent to a collection agency. Having no credit cards or credit products will not build your credit; it simply means you don't have as much credit history and therefore have less proof that you are credit worthy. Having too many credit cards, even if you don't carry a balance on them could hurt your ability to obtain a mortgage, because you may be seen as a credit risk.

Example: Steve makes $48,000 and has five credit cards of $10,000, each with no balance owing. He may think he is in great shape, but a creditor may not see it that way. Steve has the ability to rack up more credit card debt than his annual income. If Steve did spend the maximum amount on his cards, it's unlikely he would be able to pay down his principal after carrying an additional $10,000 or so in interest on his debt. One bump in the road and he is likely headed for bankruptcy.

Try not to apply for too much credit at once. If you are shopping around, applying all over for cards, you may be deemed a "credit seeker" or someone desperate for credit. The company you are applying to may start to question why you are looking for credit so desperately; they may conclude that you are about to spend it all without the intention of repaying.

Credit ratings range from 300 to 900. Anything above 700 is good, and anything above 800 is excellent. If you can get your credit score that high, you can really start to access preferential rates when you borrow.

There is a great book which elaborates on many of these issues: *Personal Finance for Canadians For Dummies*, by Eric Tyson. Everyone should read this before they get a credit card or a loan.

I can also recommend an excellent book specifically on Canadian credit. *What The Average Joe Needs To Know: The Nine Rules Of Credit*, by Richard Moxley.

MORTGAGES: A DEATH CONTRACT

Aside from investments, mortgages are the place where you can create the largest impact on your financial life. You will want to make sure you do this correctly, especially because you will likely only do it a couple of times. With mortgages, there are a few key ways to save big money. Before we delve into the ways you can save money, let's discuss whether you even need one for yourself, and then we will address how you are evaluated when you apply for a mortgage.

DO I NEED A MORTGAGE?

Many people would say, "If you are renting, you may as well throw your money in the garbage." I'm not saying these people are wrong; if you are pouring your hard earned money directly into someone else's pocket, I tend to agree in most cases. If the biggest thing you do for your finances is own your home, then good on you, but it likely isn't going to make you wealthy.

If you're not positive you are going to be living in your house for a very long time, you probably shouldn't buy it.

Instead of owning the house that I live in, I own rental property in the USA. These properties pay my rent here in Canada or wherever I am at the time. As of this writing, Canada's real estate is relatively expensive versus the real estate in the USA, and Canadian rents are relatively low compared to the value of the homes. In fact, my rent in Canada is cheaper than the cost to own the property I live in. This is usually an indicator that the price of real estate is likely to drop.

In parts of the USA, houses are very cheap and rents are relatively expensive. In fact, our tenants in Georgia are currently paying us three times the mortgage payment on average to rent our properties. The end result is that, instead of buying a house in Canada, I buy properties in America, allowing that cash-flow to pay my expenses. This is true asset purchase to fund liabilities. If you ever want to be a snowbird, buying real estate to support yourself is a great way to get that freedom quickly. For myself and my wife, there is no mortgage to support in Canada while we are away. Renting allows us much more freedom and flexibility.

This flexibility also allows us to wait patiently for when the market does change. Many of the talking heads on TV are already calling for a housing correction in Canada. An equal group of analysts are willing to argue the exact opposite. It's really hard to know when to buy a house or any investment for that matter!

To be honest, as an analyst myself, I don't pay much attention to the talking heads. There is only one thing we all know for sure; most of them are likely going to be right at some point, it's just that no one knows exactly when that is going to be.

If I were renting my house and paying my rent out of my own pocket, I could imagine feeling like I was simply tossing money away, month after month, paying someone else's mortgage. Luckily, I don't pay rent; my investment properties pay it for me. This allows me to sit back and wait comfortably until housing prices come down to the point where it begs me to snap up a great deal. When you study many of the world's most successful investors, one of the key common denominators in their strategy is patience. You can't get great deals if you are impatiently chasing them. You need to wait for them to appear and then make your move. Having rental property allows me to wait patiently and collect some nice cash flow as I bide my time.

Warren Buffett and the 20 punch card investments: Buffett suggests that one should think about investment decisions in a "punch card" fashion. He said, you will always make wiser choices if your choices are limited. You will wait for only the best opportunities and bypass the frivolous ones.

When I rent, I don't have to pay the property taxes, the insurance, or the maintenance expenses. Most importantly, if I want to move, I just move; I don't have to wait to sell my house. I don't have to pay realtors 5% of the value to sell it. I don't have to pay property transfer tax, and I can be where I want to be, when I want to be there. Currently my wife and I are "snowbirds." We spend large parts of the year in the U.S. sun belt; it's nice to be able to just leave and come back to a brand new rental property if we want. It's extremely liberating, and I believe many young people these days will want to do something similar as work becomes more flexible and mobile.

Anyhow, let's get back to mortgages.

HOW THE BANK EVALUATES YOU FOR A MORTGAGE

GDSR (GROSS DEBT SERVICE RATIO)

The first thing the bank will do when assessing you for a mortgage is look at your gross income. The reason a banker will look at your gross income, and not your net income is because people have different tax situations; gross income is the lowest common denominator across all situations. The banker will apply what's called the GDSR to your income. GDSR stands for Gross Debt Service Ratio. This is the maximum amount of money that the bank will allow you to attribute to 'servicing the debt' of a mortgage; servicing the debt means making the mortgage payment, paying property taxes, the heat bill, and half of the strata fees (if applicable). This ratio changes from bank to bank, but for our simplified example, we will use 30%.

Example: Steve makes $4,000/month. At a 30% GDSR, he will be 'allowed' to pay as much as $1,200 per month to a mortgage.

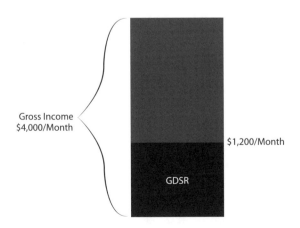

TDSR (TOTAL DEBT SERVICE RATIO)

Total Debt Service Ratio is the amount the bank will assess as the maximum portion of your gross income you can attribute to paying all your obligations to financial institutions. Some examples include: loans, lines of credit, credit cards, car payments, and your mortgage. Again, different lending institutions apply slightly different ratios, however we will use 40%.

Example: Steve is making $4,000/month and can apply $1,200 of his monthly income to the mortgage payment. However, the amount of money the bank allots to his maximum "total debt" payments is only $1,600.

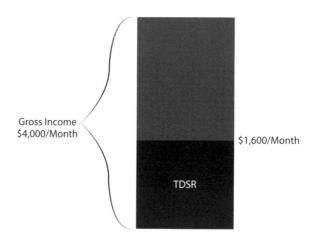

Gross Income
$4,000/Month

$1,600/Month

TDSR

THE DIFFERENTIAL/TRAP

If you have been paying attention to this point, you would have noticed that the TDSR is not much more than the GDSR, only $400. This presents a problem for the loan applicant; if the applicant has too many expenses (over the value of the differential, in our case 10%/$400), those monthly obligations start taking away from the money that could have otherwise been applied to the mortgage.

The problem many young people face is they purchase all the things they want in the near term, not thinking about what they will need in the long term. Many high school graduates that start work right out of school load up on all the toys, because they 'think' they can afford them. Fast forward 5-10 years; that debt level may prevent them from being able to own a home.

Another way they could approach this is, if they bought a cheap car to begin with, one they could pay for all at once or pay off quickly. Then, when they buy a house and put some equity into it, they could at least pull some equity out of the house to buy the car they wanted. I would never recommend this; I would recommend purchasing an investment property or other cash-flowing asset to cover the payments of the vehicle.

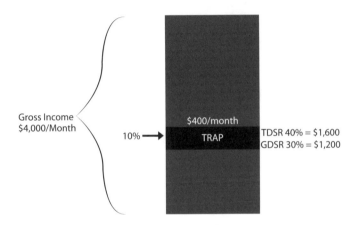

Example: Steve still makes $4,000/month; he has always felt he made enough money to afford the things he liked. He loves cars, especially American muscle cars. He bought himself a brand new Mustang GT convertible. (I would never recommend buying cars brand new off the lot, as they depreciate so quickly in the first year). Steve loves his Mustang, and that love costs him $500/month in car payments and $250 per month in insurance. He also has a credit card payment of $100/month and a LOC at $150/month . At a glance, he has recurrent monthly expenses totaling $1,000.

Breaking down Steve's situation:
Monthly Expenses = $1,000
TDSR = $1,600
Available GDSR = $600

You may be inclined to think that he can afford more than 40%. Remember, he has to pay for variable expenses such as: gas, food, dates, and all the other things that are monthly expenses. In addition, when he buys his own place, he will have to pay property transfer tax, closing fees, annual property tax, and maintenance costs. So, even if he found a $600 mortgage, he would be left with a thin margin of error when considering his other obligations. The bank wants to leave a buffer for any unforeseen events that may arise.

When you consider all of Steve's potential expenses ($1,000 tax, $1,000 bills, $600 mortgage), he is left with about $1,400/month for spending money. If we assume his variable spending is $800/month, he is left with only $600 worth of wiggle room. How is he supposed to save for the future with this kind of spending? If his down payment is less than 20% (a high ratio mortgage), he will have to pay for mortgage insurance too. I'm not sure where you live, but I'm willing to bet that you are not likely to be able to find many houses that require just a $600/month mortgage. This is what Steve's current situation looks like:

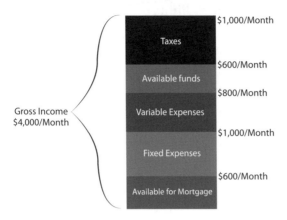

How can Steve improve his situation? If he bought a less expensive car and eliminated his credit card debt along with this line of credit, he could potentially save as much as $600/month. All of that extra cash could be contributed towards a mortgage payment, topping him up to his full GDSR of $1,200/month. If he was really savvy, he could find a place for $1,000/month, save up to be able to pay down the loan faster, and build an emergency fund for himself.

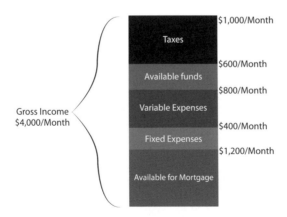

If you are considering homeownership, try to reduce your consumer debt to give yourself the best chance of a smooth and comfortable repayment. The *Canadian Mortgage Housing Corporation*[12] has a great website to educate you on the details of financial obligations.

HOW TO SAVE MONEY ON YOUR MORTGAGE

Now that we have learned a bit about how the bank evaluates you when you apply for a mortgage, let's address a couple of ways to make the pennies go further. To understand this, we have to touch on a couple of things.

MORTGAGE TERM AND AMORTIZATION PERIOD

The term of a fixed rate mortgage is the period of time that your mortgage rate is locked in before you will be forced to 'refinance' your mortgage. This means that you will have to re-visit the lender to re-negotiate the rate on your mortgage at the current rates. The rates could have gone up or down, depending on how the economy has been doing. This pushes more of the risk of future rate movements onto the Canadian borrower. The normal maximum term of a Canadian mortgage is 10 years, meaning Canadians will have to negotiate their mortgage rate at least twice. The longest amortization period available at this writing is 25 years for a "high ratio" mortgage. Conventional mortgages (20% down payment or more) can still be as long as 30 years. If the borrower is not able to save 20% for a down payment, the mortgage insurance fees can get quite high. In today's inflated price environment, it is extremely difficult for anyone living in an urban area to save for a down payment, let alone 20%.

In the USA, they still offer 30 year fixed mortgages. I'm not sure how this indicates any learning from the mistakes of the savings and loan crisis of the 1980's, but it certainly helps with real estate investing, so I'm not complaining!

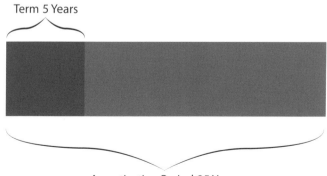

Term 5 Years

Amortization Period 25 Years

FIXED VERSUS VARIABLE RATES

This subject often stirs up deep emotion in people. I find most people get very skittish at the idea of securing themselves a variable rate mortgage. The reason for this is exactly what you would expect: people's fear of the unknown. Fixed rates are higher than variable rates, period.

So, why would you get a fixed rate? If the rates are already very low, you would get less of a discount for choosing a variable rate. If rates are historically low, you may want to lock in that low rate for as long as possible. Fixed rates do provide most people with significant peace of mind. Many older Canadians remember the early '80s when mortgage rates were in the teens or higher! At this writing, rates are very low, less than 5% for a 5 year term.

If the rates are historically high, I would advise taking a second look at variable rates. There are two reasons for this. First, the overall discount: the variable rate discount can be considerably lower than the fixed rate, so you save money right away. Second, if rates are already high, they are more likely to come down than go up. In which case, you will see a double benefit: a lower rate and a decreasing rate without a refinancing penalty.

What if rates go up? Many prospective homeowners forego a lower rate, because of the risk that it will go up. If variable rates creep above the fixed rate, you only lose the discount if the *average* rate you pay is higher than the fixed rate.

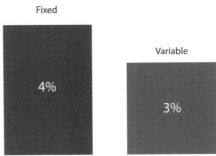

My advice would be, if you are buying in a historically low mortgage rate period, choose a longer fixed rate term, as it will secure you that lower rate for a longer time period. If rates are high, consider going shorter term and variable.

CREDIT SCORES

 We looked at credit scores in an earlier section. I can't emphasize enough how important it is to have a high credit score. Consider three simplified scenarios for a mortgage of $250,000, when the prime rate is 4%: poor credit, normal credit, and great credit.

A: Poor credit score = 500. If you get a loan, you will be penalized for your poor score via a higher mortgage rate. Let's say the penalization is 4%, your total rate is 8% for a 5 year term, 25 year amortization. When you secure a rate for the mortgage, the lender calculates the payment as if it would be the same over the entire amortization period, not just the term.

Result:
Payment = approximately $1,920/month
Total payment over 25 years = $578,862
Interest over the amortization period = $328,862

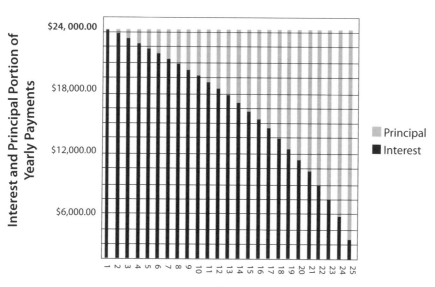

25 - Year Mortgage Payments for $250,000 Loan @ 8% Interest and Principal by Year

B: Normal credit score = 675. Resulting mortgage rate = Prime +1% or 5%

Result:
Payment = approximately $1,461/month
Total payment over 25 years = $438,442
Interest over the amortization period = $188,442

25 - Year Mortgage Payments for $250,000 Loan @ 5% Interest and Principal by Year

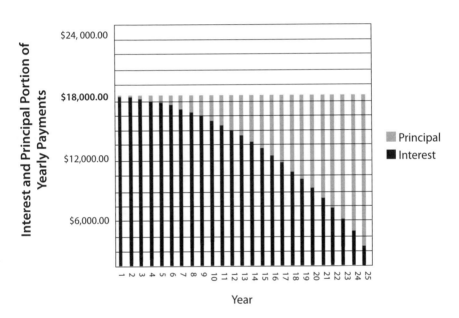

C: Great credit score = 800. Resulting mortgage rate = Prime
Result:
Payment = $1,320/month
Total payment over 25 years = $395,877
Interest over the amortization period = $145,877

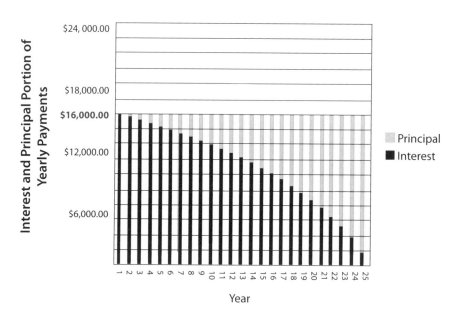

25 - Year Mortgage Payments for $250,000 Loan @ 4% Interest and Principal by Year

If you were wondering whether it is worth your time to make the effort to build and develop your credit, this example should prove that it is effort well invested. Saving hundreds of dollars a month over 25 years is worth anyone's time. You don't want to end up paying more than you need to for a home, because you neglected to pay your credit card bills on time once too often.

MORTGAGE BROKERS

 Mortgage brokers are like real estate buyers agents, incredibly useful and free to use, a very valuable asset. You do not pay a mortgage broker for their services; the lender pays them. My advice is to always use a mortgage broker; on average, they can save you about a quarter of a percent on your mortgage rate (around 25 basis points). From the examples above, you can start to see why that is such a good idea.

Mortgage brokers know of many sources of financing and the criteria of that financing. This knowledge is used to match the loan candidate with the most appropriate lender and achieve the best result.

 I recently read a fantastic book by Scott W. Peckford, a mortgage broker in Kelowna. It's called: *How to Rob Your Bank*. In this book, Peckford does a great job of explaining many ways to save money on your mortgage, in simple terms, understandable to all levels of reader.

Always get multiple opinions when you are seeking out a mortgage. This is one area where a bit more work on your end can save you big money!

PPP (PRE-PAYMENT PENALTIES)

 Pre-payment penalties are one of the ways the banks like to decrease the chance of you paying your mortgage early and thereby interrupting their steady flow of cash from your bank account. Sometimes the penalty for either paying off your mortgage early or refinancing at a lower rate, could be as much as three months interest. I advise you to read the mortgage contracts and select one that doesn't penalize you for early payments. Hint- many lenders allow a penalty free pre-payment once, annually on the anniversary of the loan.

ACCELERATED BIWEEKLY PAYMENTS

Making accelerated biweekly payments instead of monthly payments on your mortgage, is one of those jewels of wisdom that I love to give out. This particular jewel is my wife's favorite, because it is such an effortless adjustment that saves so much money.

Many people get paid every two weeks from their jobs. However, most people pay their mortgages monthly. Why is that? Is there any benefit to paying biweekly? Yes, there is a huge benefit. Most people get paid 26 times per year; you can save here by paying your mortgage on that schedule.

Because you are making 26 payments instead of 24 (as you would with a normal biweekly schedule), you are making an extra "monthly" payment per year. When you compound the effect of this payment over the life of the mortgage, it has a huge effect.

I love to play around with online maps and calculators. Online mortgage calculators are easy to find and play with. Consider visiting a link to a *mortgage calculator[13]* that compares biweekly versus monthly, or even weekly payments, and see just how much you can save by making more frequent payments.

Example:

$300,000 mortgage over 25 years @ 5% interest
Payment: $871 every two weeks instead of $1,744 every month
Cost savings (over 25 years): $37,560
Time savings: Approximately 3.7 years of payments

Payment Frequency	Payment Amount	Amortization	Term Interest Cost	Amortization Interest Cost	Amortization Interest Savings vs. Monthly Payment
Monthly	$1,744.82	25.0 yrs	$223,443.02	$223,443.02	$0.00
Bi-weekly	$805.30	24.9 yrs	$220,571.04	$220,571.04	$2,871.98
Accelerated Bi-weekly	$872.41	21.4 yrs	$185,882.99	$185,882.99	$37,560.03

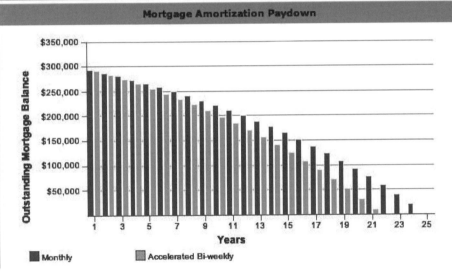

Chapter 3
Money Love: Money Making Money

"Compound interest is the eighth wonder of the world. He who understands it, earns it ... he who doesn't ... pays it." - Albert Einstein

COMPOUND INTEREST

Compounding interest can happen when you lend or invest money; the money grows quickly, because the interest or return gains interest as well.

First let's define some terms:

Principal: The original amount of money loaned or invested.
Interest: Money paid to the owner of the money for its use.
Compounding interest: When you gain interest on previous interest, as well as the principal.

When most people think about an interest payment, they consider the amount of principal owed and multiply it by the interest rate to find how much the interest is. This is an example of simple interest. Compounding interest is one step more complex.

When you compound interest, for every year that you owe interest in the past, you must add this to the total amount owing. This combines the original loan with the previous interest owed from each subsequent year.

Example: Steve loans $100 to a friend. The loan is carried at 10% interest, with the principal and all interest payable in 3 years.

SIMPLE INTEREST

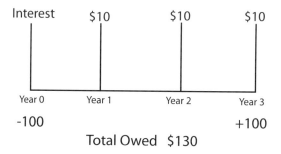

Year 0 = Loan made for $100
Year 1 = Interest accrued = ($100 x 10%) = $10
Year 2 = Interest accrued = ($100 x 10%) = $10
Year 3 = Interest accrued = ($100 x 10%) = $10

Total interest owed = $30
Principal repayment = $100
Total owed at year 3 = $130

COMPOUNDING INTEREST

Total Owed $133.10

Year 0 = Loan made $100
Year 1 = Interest accrued = ($100 x 10%) = $10
Year 2 = Interest accrued = ($110 x 10%) = $11
        (in this year, $110 is used instead of $100)
Year 3 = Interest accrued = ($121 x 10%) = $12.10
        (in this year, $121 is used instead of $100)

Total interest owed = $ 33.10
Repayment = $100
Total owed at year 3 = $133.10

In this short example, it may be challenging to quickly identify the big deal here. It seems like compounding the interest, or gaining interest on interest nets you very little extra money. However, as you continue this pattern further out into the future, it becomes a very big deal.

If you were to continue this pattern for 30 years, the final numbers would be:

Simple: $100 + Interest of $300 = Total $400
Compound: $100 + Interest $1,744.94 = Total $1,844.94

Here is what this looks like on a graph:

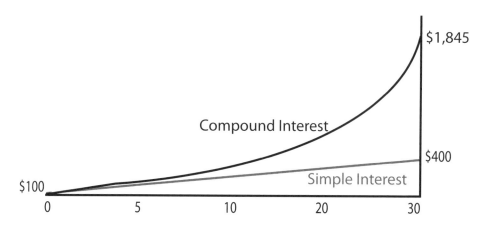

The way in which you find the future value of any loan by compounding over time is one of the most basic calculations in finance, and the one I learned first. This is the formula for those of you who want to tinker with it:

$FV = PV(1 + i)^n$
FV = Future value
PV = Present value
i = Interest rate
n = Number of periods. In our case the interest was counted yearly. However, we could calculate monthly, in which case we would have to change the interest rate to 10%/12.

In our example, the numbers were: FV = $100(1+.1)^{30}$ = 1774.94
If you would rather have the calculation done for you, feel free to use an online calculator like this one from *Money Chimp*.[14]

RULE OF 72

If you want to learn how to quickly estimate these numbers in your head, you can use the "rule of 72." The rule of 72 says that if you multiply the number of years you invest by the average rate of return, when the equation hits 72, you will double your money.

Example:

Using $10,000, we will run through a couple of examples.
(12 x 6 = 72): 12 years investing at 6% = $20,122
(6 x 12 = 72): 6 years investing at 12% = $19,738
(10 x 7.2 = 72): 10 years investing at 7.2% = $20,042
(7.2 x 10 = 72): 7.2 years investing at 10% = $19,862

This is where the rubber meets the road in your financial life. The long term average return on the stock market is about 10%. With what you have just learned, you can start to play with the math to project your future wealth.

If you started investing at age 30, how much money will you have if you retire at age 65? Could you save more money and retire earlier? Could you gain more interest or returns to retire faster? Which one is easier, saving and investing more up front, or finding higher returns? We will explore the answers to these questions in chapter 5.

Chapter 4

The Stock Market: Water Cooler Talk

"The main purpose of the stock market is to make fools of as many men as possible." - Bernard Baruch

Before we delve into the details of what I will call "water cooler talk," take a moment to think about the ways you can invest your money. Invariably, the stock market will rank as one of the first things most people think about as an investment vehicle. While this is the most popular by far, stock market investing is not the most effective way to achieve financial freedom (more on this in chapter 8). Also, if history continues on the current path, stocks will become less and less effective in making money for investors. However, it is important for everyone to understand the basics of how this market works, if only to add it to your options as a vehicle for wealth creation.

It is important to have a working knowledge of whichever vehicle you choose to grow your money. You must understand what you invest in; the easiest way to lose your money is to fail to understand your investment.

WHAT IS A STOCK?

A stock is a small piece of ownership in a company. If a company was cut up like one of those huge Costco cakes, each square would represent a share in the company. It means that as an 'owner' of the company, you participate in both the profits and losses of the company. You also have a voice in how the company is run. You are able to attend the AGM (Annual General Meeting) to hear from the company executives about how the company has performed, and you are privy to the plans for the future. You are able to vote for the addition of a new board and the management.

In most cases you buy stocks in the stock market. This is the place where shares of companies "change hands" many times per day. Physical trading floors, like this one depicted at the New York Stock Exchange, have been largely replaced by electronic trading systems. Whether physical or virtual, this exchange of ownership is performed on the **secondary market**.

There is another market where you are able to buy stock in a company. The **primary market** is where a stock is bought or 'issued' for the very first time. Unfortunately, this primary market is typically accessible only to wealthy investors, so poor average Joe misses out.

WHERE DO STOCKS COME FROM?

The life cycle of a company can follow a few different paths. However, the goal of many companies is to grow to a size that warrants selling ownership in the company to the general public. This is called an IPO or initial public offering.

IPOs are handled by investment bankers; these are the guys who look like they are from the movies, with the slick hair to match their slick suits (think Christian Bale, in the movie "American Psycho"). These are the men who buy and sell whole companies, all the while making gobs of money. An investment banker will perform all the necessary research and file all the appropriate forms to list a company for sale to the public for the first time. The price at which they end up selling the stock, well... let's just say there is a lot of educated guessing going on. Eventually, the market will tell them how close they were to the mark. These bankers will also play a hand in distributing the shares to the first buyers.

Luckily for us normal folk, we don't have to worry about those sometimes pesky bankers and their hot new investment opportunities, because they have a specific type of client in mind when they want to sell their wares: the wealthy. This first round of opportunity often goes directly to the high net worth clients at the full service brokerages and the institutional investors (buying for mutual funds, foundations, and **endowments**). In layman's terms, the rich people get first crack at buying the hot new stocks, but don't worry yourself about missing out on opportunities. Buying IPOs can be riskier than buying regular stock. There are good ones and an equal amount of bad ones, but no way to tell which is which.

WHAT GIVES A STOCK ITS VALUE?

There are many measures of a stock's value, which can be conflicting and confusing at times. For instance, from my description above, a stock's value should be equivalent to how big the pie or cake is. This would be the stock's **book value**. Alternatively, you could apply any number of increasingly complex valuation models (or equations) that will spit back at you a certain number of what the value 'should' be. I will briefly describe one of the most popular valuation formulas for you. I know we have made it this far with no serious mathematics, and I intend to continue on that path. I will also let you in on a little secret; in functional finance, you don't need to exercise much higher math skill than you would in 10th grade algebra. Here is the very popular **Dividend Discount Model (DDM)** of stock valuation.

$D_1/K\text{-}g$
D_1 = Dividend in the first period
K = Discount rate
g = Internal growth rate of the company

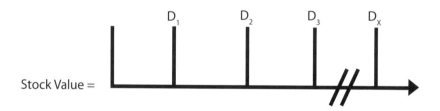

This image of a time line is the single most valuable tool for almost any investment problem. No matter how you structure the question, the problem boils down to: where the money is and when, how fast it is growing, the length of time, and the discount factor. You will see how useful it is to repeatedly draw out a picture like this, over and over again, depending on the situation.

I like to explain the idea of DDM by starting at the end. People often have trouble imagining the value of a stock by the sum of its future dividends. However, they find it less complex to imagine interest owed on money in a bank account.

Imagine you had $100 in a special bank account. This bank account paid you interest at 10% per year. You intend to keep that $100 right where it is forever, always spending the $10, and never saving it (g=0). If this were the case, you would have $100, paying you $10 per year, forever.

Let's look at that exact situation in reverse. Imagine you were paid $10 per year, every year, forever. How much would all those $10 bills be worth to you today if the interest rate you could get at the bank was 10%? (K=10%)

Some people find it difficult to wrap their heads around the fact that all those $10 payments are only worth $100. However, remember that they aren't worth $10 in the present; they must be "discounted" to the present value.

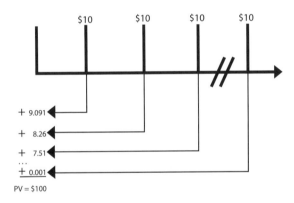

As with our example of the deposit in the bank, the value of the stock according to the DDM is simply the sum of the present value of all the future dividends. The abbreviation of this long number line is the formula I started with. Is this really that complex?

As a 'higher level' topic, imagine what would happen if a company that was paying regular dividends for decades, suddenly cut its dividend to 90% of what it used to be. By our model/formula the DDM, that would have a huge impact due to the fact that all future payouts past the date of the dividend change would need to be adjusted. The sum of all those changes could cause a pretty dramatic change in the current price of the stock.

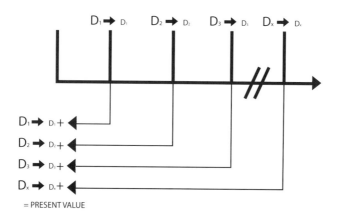

Sometimes the stock changes wildly in price for other reasons. Sometimes the company doesn't even pay a dividend. That is why many experienced traders and investors will tell you that at the end of the day, the value of a stock is the price someone is willing to pay you for it. In the short term, I think that saying is very true. Warren Buffett, arguably the world's most famous and most successful investor, explains that in the long term, the stock market is like a weighing machine, logically weighing the information in the market and determining the value of the stock accordingly. In the short term, it's like a voting machine, tallying up the people who want to buy versus sell.

Stock Market in the Long Term   Stock Market in the Short Term

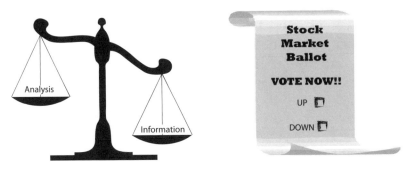

WHAT ARE SOME OF THE PROS AND CONS OF OWNING STOCKS?

PROS

A vote in company affairs

Profit participation

Dividends

Capital gains

Something to talk about

CONS

Changing values (volatility)

Participation in losses

Systematic (market) risk

Taxes

Company specific risk

I would like to comment on the last item on each list. First, the water cooler talk; do not laugh- for many people, this is by far the biggest pro of investing in the stock market. Everyone loves to talk about the stock market, don't they? It even has its own section in the newspaper. It's fast paced and it's exciting. People love dropping comments to let you know that they have a broker or investment advisor to tell them what to do with their money. My point is people love to talk about the market like it is a soap opera. Who's up? Who's down? Who's winning this month? Who lost big? I admit that it can be quite entertaining, even exciting. But keep in mind that this is just one of the many ways to invest, and it's very tough to successfully play in the same sandbox as the masses.

If you would like to chance your arm at a little stock picking, you can always try to do some mock trading on a stock trading simulation game. One that I found fairly comprehensive can be found on *Investopedia.*[15] You can give yourself a virtual million dollars and trade against your friends. It's always fun, especially once you learn about derivatives (later). While it can be great entertainment, for the average investor, trying to pick stocks is a fools errand.

TWO TYPES OF RISK

There are two main types of risk an investor bears when they buy a stock: company specific or idiosyncratic risk and overall market risk.

Company specific risk is exactly that, risk that is particular to that company. If the company CEO passes away unexpectedly, there is likely to be an effect on that one stock, but not many others as a result. Alternatively, should there be a terrorist attack on a major world financial centre, the effect would be broad, affecting the entire market.

If you are going to invest in the stock market, you are going to bear market risk; you can't escape it. However, you can escape idiosyncratic or company specific risk through diversification. This is the main reason the word 'diversify' is so popular in the mutual fund world. As shown by the chart, when a portfolio reaches 23-30 stocks, the positive and negative effects of the various random company events more or less cancel each other out, and you are left with only market risk.

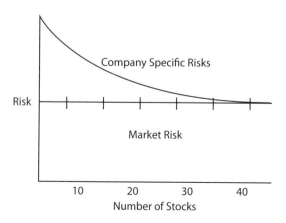

Look at any actively managed mutual fund; it will likely consist of 20-30 stocks. The reason for this is diversification; it sounds like a good idea on the surface. However, this "diversification" is the first thing at which you should raise your eyebrow. As we continue our discussion about risk to incorporate reward, you will see why this strategy that keeps portfolios "safe" from undue risk also keeps them from outperforming.

A more in-depth analysis of this can be found in almost any entry level finance text book. If you are interested in deepening your knowledge in this area, look up terms like: beta, alpha, and **security market line** on the internet.

 Let's focus on the big picture without getting unnecessarily academic. If a portfolio/mutual fund is fully diversified, it is only exposed to market wide risk. It therefore has some ratio of risk exposure compared to the entire stock market (this exposure is called beta). Equivalent risk level would result in an equivalent return. I'm sorry if I have burst anyone's bubble with this simple revelation, and I am certainly not the first to realize this, but many fund managers and salespeople would love to make sure you never took an interest in learning this very simple idea. I expand on this topic in the next chapter.

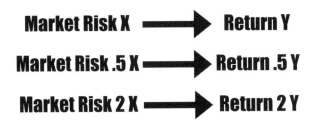

If you are "fully diversified,"
you get the return that matches your risk level.

Chapter 5

Mutual Funds: Buyer Beware

"If stock market experts were so expert, they would be buying stock, not selling advice." - Norman Ralph Augustine

WHAT IS A MUTUAL FUND?

A mutual fund is an investment product made up of a pool of funds collected from many investors for the purpose of investing in a collection of stocks and bonds. The stocks are selected by analysts. The manager, likely a former analyst himself, is an experienced professional. Investing in a mutual fund will give you cheap diversification. What do I mean by "cheap diversification?" Imagine you want to buy 30 stocks to get fully diversified; that would mean 30 purchases. Even at $20 commission per purchase, that's $600 in commission just to buy your stocks. If you only have $10,000, that could be a problem. Also, you probably won't be able to buy 100 shares of each stock. 100 shares is a typical **board lot**; any odd number is called an **odd lot**. If you are purchasing an odd lot, your commissions (the money you pay the broker to buy the shares) will likely increase.

So now that we know what a mutual fund provides us, what do we pay for this convenience? If there is one thing I want to say about mutual funds it's that Canadian management fees are entirely too high to provide any added value to the purchaser. There are a few types of fees you need to be aware of.

FEES

If you are forced to invest using mutual funds, you should learn how to do it as intelligently as possible. By reducing the fees, you automatically increase the returns. If you reduce the cost to buy a mutual fund by 1%, you've increased your return by 1%.

MANAGEMENT EXPENSE RATIO (MER)

This is the fee that every mutual fund charges to invest in the fund. It includes all the ongoing fees of the fund: the manager's fee, the costs to print the **prospectus** and annual reports, custodial fees, the costs to mail statements, and even the federal and provincial regulatory fees. It also includes the trailer fee that is paid to your advisor. The MER represents most of the expenses of a fund, expressed as a percentage of the value of the investment.

A typical MER on an "actively" managed Canadian equity fund is about 2.5%. This means the fund company takes 2.5% of investors' money annually, to cover their cost to manage the fund and to make a profit. If you invest $10,000 into a fund with a 2.5% MER, you are paying $250 per year in fees. If you invest $100,000 into a fund, you're paying the fund company $2,500 per year, regardless of the performance of the fund. Win or lose, they get their money. **In my opinion, not only is this percentage too high, but it is unfair to the client who makes the larger investment and receives the same service.**

 This is the most important fee to pay attention to, because it can vary significantly from fund to fund. It is paid directly from your assets in the fund and can greatly affect the return whether you see it or not!

TRANSACTION FEES

The second type of fee to understand is the commission fee when you either buy or sell a mutual fund; these are called "selling fees" or "commissions." Funds that charge fees to buy or sell are called "loaded" funds.

There are three ways that advisors sell loaded funds: on a deferred-sales-charge basis (DSC), on a front-end basis (FE), or on a low-load basis (LL).

DEFERRED SALES CHARGE (DSC)

This is a sneaky fee! A fund purchased using the deferred-sales-charge option charges the client no up front commission, but there is a charge when selling the fund in the first 5 to 7 years you own it. Thus, the deferred part of "deferred sales charge." The actual fee to sell the fund depends on the length of time you keep it and the fee schedule of that particular fund company. Most fund companies have DSC schedules that are 6 to 7 years long, start at 5% to 6%, and decline to zero over that period.

What your advisor isn't likely to tell you about DSC fees is that, some fund companies charge this fee based on your invested amount; others charge this fee based on the market value. This might seem like an insignificant detail, but it isn't.

What's the big difference between a DSC schedule based on market value versus one based on invested value?

Example: Last year, Steve invested $10,000 in a mutual fund with a deferred-sales charge based on his invested value. His advisor explained the DSC schedule and gave him a copy which looks like this:

Year of Redemption	Redemption Fee
During the first year of buying	5.5%
During the second year after buying	5.5%
During the third year after buying	5.0%
During the fourth year after buying	4.5%
During the fifth year after buying	4.0%
During the sixth year after buying	3.0%
During the seventh year after buying	1.5%
After seven years of buying	Zero

Over the past 13 months, Steve's fund has fallen sharply. Down by more than 40%, the market value is slightly less than $6,000. He decides he can't handle further declines and decides to sell. A little more than a year has passed since the purchase, so he expects fees of 5.5% to sell. However, when Steve bought the fund, his advisor didn't explain that the redemption fee is based on invested value.

He invested $10,000. His deferred-sales fee is based on this amount. The fee for selling during the second year is 5.5%, which is $550 (5.5% x $10,000). Because the account value is only $6,000, his real redemption fee is closer to 9% ($550 fee on a $6,000 sale). Before you buy a DSC mutual fund, ask if the fees are based on market value or invested value. DSC funds are becoming less and less common. My advice would be to simply avoid any fund with a back end load fee or DSC, unless you are 100% certain you won't sell early. The UK and Australia have effectively banned DSC funds because of the misalignment between advisor and client.

FRONT-END FEES (FE)

The financial industry lacks imagination; For the most part, everything is exactly what it says it is. That's a good thing, because investing is hard enough! Front-end fees are exactly what they sound like: fees to get into the investment at the front end. With this option, you're charged a fee (commission) when you buy and not charged when you sell. This front-end fee will reduce the value of your investment from 1% to 5% immediately, but is completely negotiable with your advisor. This is one of those times when it pays to be a good negotiator. Financial advisors will almost always sell you the investment at a lower fee if pressed. Most advisors try to charge the maximum (5%) and quickly retreat downward if the client calls them out on it. Too many investors say nothing and pay whatever their advisor asks. If you have to buy a mutual fund, my suggestion is to never pay more than 2% up front. Remember financial professionals compete for your business.

LOW-LOAD SALES OPTION (LL)

The low-load option is a deferred-sales schedule that is less punitive than the full DSC: 2 to 3 years rather than 6 to 7 years. Think of it as "DSC mini." You pay no commission to purchase the fund, and you're not stuck in a 7-year commitment. Not only is your money completely fee-free to withdraw after fewer years, the fees are far less. Here's an example of a low-load schedule:

Low-Load Sales Charge Option

Securities sold during the following period after you bought them	Redemption Fee Rate
during the first year	3.0%
during the second year	2.5%
during the third year	2.0%

Regardless of what commission you pay, your financial advisor is paid an annual trailer fee from the fund company to service your account. Servicing your account means meeting with you at least once per year to discuss your investment strategy. Often, people enter these meetings feeling confused and leave feeling overwhelmed and more confused. The gross trailer fee that is paid to keep you invested is generally between .5% and 1% of your investment.

Example: If you invest $10,000 into a mutual fund, your advisor can earn $100 per year to service you. The point is, your investment provides ongoing income for your financial planner, without him having to charge you a visible yearly fee. This is money that could have otherwise been growing.

NO-LOAD FUNDS

A no-load fund means exactly that: no front-end load, no back-end load, only a trailer fee (which is paid out of the MER). It has two benefits: zero fees to buy or sell and a much lower MER. The reason for this reduced fee is that no compensation is paid to the seller.

Always keep in mind that the person selling actively managed mutual funds is paid by the mutual fund company. Their compensation may influence which products they present to you. Often, these people have more sales training than independent investment education. Your self-education is your best investment!

Some people have no choice but to invest through a mutual fund, because of the way their pension is set up. I personally do not, have not, and will never invest in an actively managed mutual fund; the reasons for this are many, but I will summarize it for you.

It is possible to prove that the <u>managers of mutual funds typically do not add any value to the investment performance.</u> In fact, if anything they take away returns with their high fees. <u>Planners can add value to the overall process through education and guidance to keep you on the correct path over the years.</u> This guidance does come at a very steep cost, which I display for you next.

I encourage you to do your own research on this topic; it is to your direct benefit. Read this short article, *Mission Improbable by Ken French*[16], one of the forefathers of finance, to learn more about the likelihood of beating the market. Hopefully, my examples will get you thinking about the true cost of these fees and the manager's advice/professional management.

Examples:
In our first example, Steve has saved $40,000 in his RRSP. He wants to approximate how much his savings will grow before he retires at age 65.

He intends to place it all in the stock market, through an actively managed mutual fund with a financial advisor at the bank. He will not contribute to the account after he invests the initial $40,000.

Age 30
Initial investment = $40,000 (no more contributions after that)
Rate of return= 8% (10% average stock market return-2% fee)
Time horizon= 35 years
Future value = $591,000

What would happen if Steve paid no fee at all, but got the same return on his investment?

Age 30
Savings = $40,000 (no more contributions after that)
Rate of return=10%
Time horizon= 35 years
Future value = $1,124,000

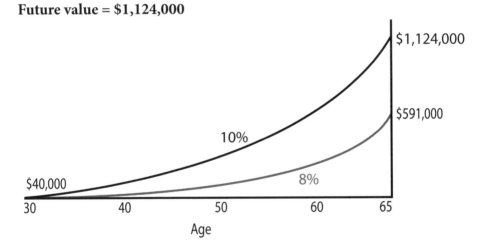

 That's a big difference; over 35 years, the difference of a 2% return generated almost twice as much money. The reason for this is the 2% fee he pays every year; that is 2% less money that can grow over time. When you take capital away to pay a fee, that is called a hard cost. When you lose the ability to gain returns on the lost capital, that is called "**opportunity cost.**" In our example above, Steve pays more than $100,000 in fees and more than $400,000 in opportunity cost.

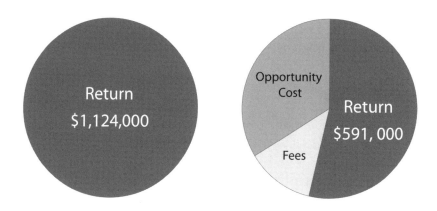

 When you invest in a Canadian mutual fund, you are going to pay a MER (management expense ratio). Canadian firms are notorious for their high fees! The *Ontario Securities Commission*[17] has created a wonderful tool, which allows you to calculate the fees for any mutual fund sold in Canada.

What about saving more? How much more money would Steve have to start with to make up for the 2% return lost to fees?

Age 30
Future value = $1,124,000
Rate of return= 8% (10%-2% fee)
Time horizon= 35 years
Initial investment = $76,000

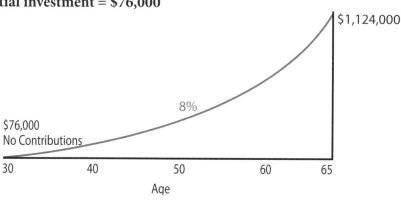

This means to make up for the extra costs from fees, Steve would have to have saved $76,000 before making the initial investment. That's $36,000 (90%) more money saved to compensate for the fees.

If you are getting 8% instead of 10% returns, you would have to have almost double the amount of money to start with, to make up for the difference of just the fee. I would rather find lower fees than try to save twice as much money.

If Steve started with no savings at age 30, how much would he need to save and invest every year for 35 years at 10% return to get to the same $1,124,097.48?

Age 30
Future value = $1,124,097.48
Rate of return= 10%
Time horizon= 35 years
Savings = 0
Yearly payments = $4,147.58 per year for 35 years

If he is starting with $0 at age 30 instead of $40,000, he would have to save $4,147 per year for all 35 years, instead of $4,000 per year from age 20-30. I would rather save the smaller amount for 10 years than the larger amount for 35 years, wouldn't you?

What if Steve were able to have saved just $25,000 by age 25 and put that to work without fees at 10% until age 65? This yields $1,132,000: over a million dollars for just $25,000 invested in your younger years.

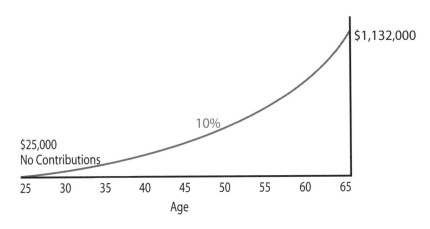

At age 20, Steve gets a $15,000 inheritance. What is this worth if he can compound at 10% until age 65 without fees? $1,093,000.

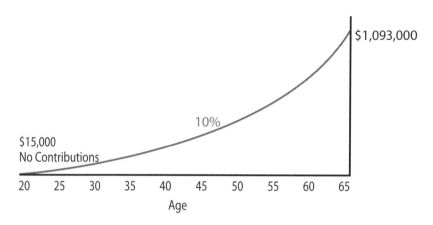

Every way you cut it, time is always the most important in your younger years. Starting to invest at a young age takes a massive amount of stress off the investor in later years. Another observation is that you need to make sure you're not paying a fraction of a percent more in fees than is absolutely necessary. Finally, you want to make sure that you are achieving the highest returns possible. The 5 million dollar question is, "How do I get high returns without higher risk?" We will discuss this in chapter 8, but just for fun, let's do one more example pretending we could find an investment that would yield 15% per year. How much money would we have at the end?

Age 30
Investment = $40,000 (no contributions afterward)
Rate of return= 15%
Time horizon= 35 years
Future value = $5,327,020.94

This book is dedicated to helping you understand how to save yourself money so that you can make wise investment decisions. If you use this book as the passport it was designed to be, you will be able to find higher return investments and see them for what they are: pure gold.

In summary, saving 'more' at an early age doesn't seem to have nearly as large an impact as cutting down the fees and getting higher returns. It's much easier to find low fee investments than it is to find something that will consistently pay you 10% or more. The stock market average has been about 10% over the last 50 years or so. It's not too difficult to find a better return than that, but you have to know where to look. You have to take control, and take action when you find it, but more on this later.

 Check out the *OSC's interactive chart*[18] for historical performance of the different markets.

I mentioned before how I love to play with online maps and calculators. A personal favorite of mine is an *online retirement savings calculator.*[19] Nowhere does the power of compounding show more clearly than on a tool like this. Try this one out, and see how much money you could have if you started putting your money to work!

CAN A MUTUAL FUND BEAT THE STOCK MARKET?

The problem is not so much that a fund can't beat the market. Actually, about 15% of funds beat the market on a net performance basis in any single year. However, it has been empirically proven that it is almost impossible to beat the market consistently overtime.

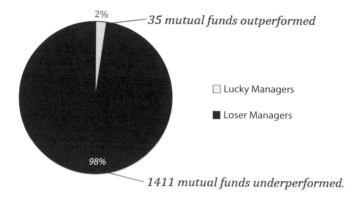

Ten Years Ending October 2004
Large Cap Mutual Funds vs S&P 500 Index

2% —*35 mutual funds outperformed*

☐ Lucky Managers

■ Loser Managers

98%

— *1411 mutual funds underperformed.*

SOURCE: TWINCITIES.COM

BIG DEAL The chances of the same fund beating the market 5 years in a row are pretty slim. What's more, if a fund does out perform over 5 years, it's even more likely to underperform over the subsequent 5 years. If you look at 10 year time periods, the chance of market outperformance is less than 3%. Also, it's near impossible to predict which fund will outperform in any year, but people do love to try, because they get paid to do it! In fact, there is a multi-billion dollar industry supporting the attempts of people trying to beat the market and the promotion of their efforts.

There are more mutual funds trading today than there are stocks. There are many different ways that analysts and fund managers can dice up the market to try to gain exposure to a particular niche. For example, they can divvy the market by size and only buy **small cap stocks**. They can choose a particular **sector** to focus on, such as energy. They can focus on a style of investing, like value or growth. Likely, they are going to be a combination of all three. There are a lot of different possible combinations, and when you mix in the various levels of bond exposure to these funds, and consider that many mutual fund companies have competing products, you can imagine why there are more mutual funds than there are stocks.

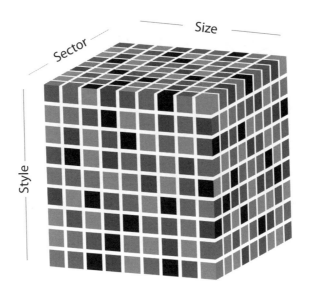

THE PARADOX OF RESEARCH

Research and common sense both tell us that with the millions of people involved in building, supporting, and marketing mutual funds, they more or less **are** the market. Therefore they can't reasonably expect to beat themselves at their own game. The result is a landscape that enables anyone to pick stocks randomly and perform virtually as well as a professional mutual fund manager. There has been more than one study on this random selection versus professional manager. I'm sorry to say the managers haven't fared so well.

"A blindfolded monkey throwing darts at a newspaper's financial pages could select a portfolio that would do just as well as one carefully selected by experts" - Burton Malkiel, Author - *A Random Walk Down Wall Street* and leading proponent of the Efficient Market Hypothesis.

However, what would happen if the analysts and managers stopped doing their research. What if there were no one doing any investment research? What would happen to the mutual fund industry? Well, ironically, if no one did any research, then research would be extremely valuable, because few people would have it. Currently, with so much research around, it adds very little value.

In the investment world, there is a theory called the **efficient market hypothesis** (make sure to work this into conversations at parties if you would like to increase your popularity). The EMH states that the financial markets are stable and kept in efficient balance, because of the large amount of research being done. The research is what keeps the risk and return balanced throughout the market.

Obviously, some companies are riskier than others. Therefore, the potential reward for investing in riskier companies should be proportionately higher. One of the mechanisms that allow us to observe this in action is called the **security market line**. This line is the very definition of the risk/reward relationship between stocks.

All stocks theoretically rest on the line. Should a stock deviate upward or downward, by increasing or decreasing in value, it is pushed back onto the line (and back into risk/reward alignment) with the rest of the stocks. Stocks get pushed up and down by the buying and selling pressure of the stock on the market. A plotting above the line or positive alpha, means the stock is undervalued, and therefore, analysts recommend purchasing the stock until it comes back down on to the line; the opposite is also true. If a stock plots

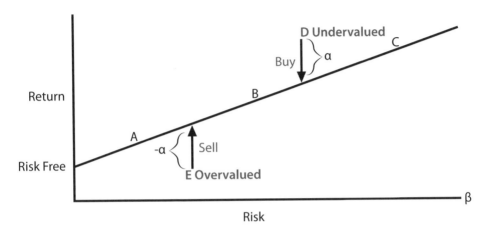

below the line, it is sold off, the stock's price drops due to lack of demand, and it floats back in line with the rest of the market.

Many analysts are paid large salaries to identify which stocks are off the line and buy or sell them accordingly, to capture as much "extra" return or "alpha" as possible. Without these analysts doing their jobs and often over doing it (if you know any analysts, you know they are tied to their work), the market would be much less efficient. Ironically, if the market were much less efficient, it would be easier to beat the market average. Alas, the analysts actually do perform a function, and it's unlikely that this will stop in the near future.

These analysts are usually educated at the finest schools and are professionally trained by the most profitable banks and brokerages in the world. Some "normal" people do try to beat the analysts at their own game. While it isn't impossible to beat them at times, I don't recommend trying. It's not that I don't like the challenge, I simply prefer to compete when the odds are stacked in my favor.

So, if the market is efficient, does investing in a mutual fund that will perform the same as most other mutual funds make any sense at all? In my opinion, it doesn't make sense to pay for the benefit of research if you can get it for free! How do you use their efforts for free? You can buy a fund or product that uses their work for free. They are called ETFs and index funds.

SOCIALLY RESPONSIBLE INVESTING

Many years ago, when I was first designing the curriculum for my course, I worked with a colleague named Michelle. She exemplified a charitable spirit, and we got along very well. She always encouraged me to bring as much ethical influence as possible to the subject of wealth and investing. It is with her in mind that I include this section.

Socially responsible investing is a growing topic in finance. Some funds avoid investing in companies that promote, manufacture, or distribute firearms, military goods, tobacco, gambling, and other morally questionable goods and services. If you have the intention of bringing your values to your investments, consider investing in socially responsible funds.

IF MUTUAL FUNDS CAN'T BEAT THE MARKET OVER TIME, WHAT IS THE ALTERNATIVE?

I have always been a "big picture" person. When I think about the mutual fund world and its lack of performance, especially in the first ten years of the 21st century (the "lost decade"), I get slightly depressed. So many people started investing their money and ten years later had less than they did when they started. What's worse, the reason they have lost money in a flat market is, because they were losing 2% or more on average in fees! Throughout this period, billions of dollars left the mutual fund world and headed towards do-it-yourself discount brokerages, index funds, and ETFs.

WHAT IS AN ETF OR INDEX FUND?

 ETF stands for exchange-traded fund; this product electronically matches whatever it is you want to track. The best part about this tool is that it typically has an extremely low MER because there is no human manager. As we have seen time and time again, human managers stick to the herd and overtime fail to beat the index. So why not buy the entire index? An index fund is defined as a type of mutual fund, with a portfolio constructed to match or track the components of a market index, such as the S&P 500. For our purposes, index funds and ETFs will mean the same thing.

ETFs can be selected and segmented in the same way as mutual funds: by size, sector, style (value or growth), geographically, and the list goes on. They are also more flexible than mutual funds; they can be bought and sold during the day, they can be short sold, or they can be bought on **margin**.

If I was looking for diversification or forced to invest my retirement in the stock market, I would choose to invest in ETFs and not give my hard earned money and returns to a manager that can't beat the index. I would be in good company in my decision; many pillars of the financial community would agree with me. Take a look at some of their comments:

Peter Lynch, manager of the famous Fidelity Magellan fund: *"Most investors would be better off with an index fund."*

Jonathan Clements, author of *Little Book of Main Street Money* and Director of Financial Education for Citi Personal Wealth Management: *"Most investors are pretty smart... Yet, most investors remain invested in actively managed stock funds."*

Burton Malkiel, author of *A Random Walk Down Wall Street* and Director at Vanguard: *"Why does indexing out-maneuver the best minds at wall street? Paradoxically, it is because the best and the brightest of the financial community have made the stock market very efficient."*

William Bernstein, American financial theorist: *"It turns out, for all practical purposes, there is no such thing as stock picking skill..."*

Ron Ross, Economist: *"Active management is little more than a gigantic con game."*

William F. Sharpe, Nobel Laureate in Economics: *"Most of my investments are in equity index funds."*

Warren Buffett, most famous successful investor of the 20th century and CEO of Berkshire Hathaway: *"..the best way to own common stocks is through an index fund that charges minimal fees."*

If there is anyone's advice you should follow regarding investments, I would recommend you take the advice of the people who designed, studied, and mastered the art of investing. Your local bank or Investco employee...well they may need a few more years to catch up.

I am aware that at this stage I am telling you to stay away from mutual funds, and instead go with ETFs or index funds. I'm not telling you which index funds to invest in, and I'm not telling you when to invest. I will pay more attention to this topic later. For now, we need to collect information on where the pitfalls lie, and then move on to how to avoid them. We need to know where to gather information to tailor to our own path. There is no "one size fits all" plan waiting for you at the end of the book. You may be "forced" to invest in the market as a function of your company sponsored pension plan, or your RRSP, or other tax deferred plan. If that's the case, you want to make the wisest decisions possible.

The stock market is not the sand box in which you want to compete with the professionals. In my opinion, given the returns, I don't understand why people still pay so much attention to this market at all. In the future, actively managed mutual fund investors and advisors will become as numerous as smokers; there are some stubborn ones around, but you rarely have to think about them.

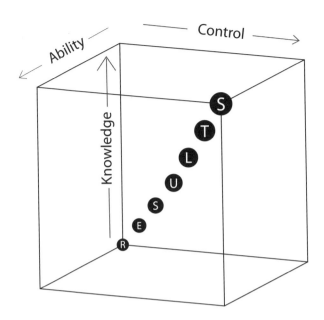

The stock market is one of the least efficient tools in wealth generation. Your success in wealth creation will be a direct result of three positively related factors: how much knowledge you have, your ability to put that information to work for you, and how much control you have over the outcome. No one else will take care of your retirement or wealth planning like you will. I'm aware that most people will not be their own **pension fund** managers, but if I can contribute to helping the investing public to make smarter decisions, this book will have served its purpose. In chapter 8, we will discuss a few other sandbox options in which to play.

Chapter 6
Fixed Income Products

"I did the thing with bonds, which was about $30 million and I didn't get none of the money on them." - James Brown

With all this discussion about stocks, we have completely forgotten about bonds. There is a good reason for this: complete lack of "water cooler talk." You have to be in some very nerdy circles for people to be working bond performance into party conversations. I don't generally recommend investing in public bonds, but it's important to know a few things about them.

What do we really know about bonds? What is a bond anyway? How big is the bond market? If the bond market really is six times the size of the stock market, why doesn't it occupy six times the amount of space in the newspaper?

WHAT IS A BOND?

A bond is a loan to a government or corporation. When you loan money in this way, you are paid interest for the use of your money. For example, you may loan money to the Canadian government, and they might pay you 5% interest for 30 years. At the end of 30 years, you get your money back with your final interest payment.

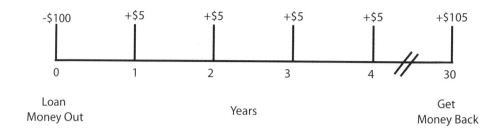

Governments borrow money all the time, for all sorts of reasons. One of the reasons for borrowing money is to finance war. Many people may have heard of or even remember "victory bonds" or "war bonds." Corporations may borrow money to build a new factory or store.

Unlike a stock or share, a bond is a loan and therefore is not 'ownership' of that company. The owner of a bond is not entitled to a say in how the company is run, nor a participation in the profits or losses. A bond owner is simply a silent collector of interest.

Because bond owners only collect interest and not profit, their return on investment is often much more stable. Unfortunately, the returns go down with risk, and so bond holders don't make much money. In fact, they make so little money, it may be worthwhile to figure out if one should invest in bonds at all.

The average long-term bond fund would have returned approximately 7.5% from 1950-2011 (as per the Canadian 2011 Andex® Chart). It's important to realize that long term bonds typically return higher than short term or medium term bonds. So, these numbers are a bit top heavy to begin with. Regardless, 7.5% almost sounds attractive, except for two major problems.

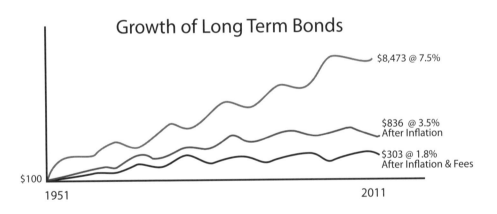

Problem 1: If you look at the 2011 Andex® Chart, you will see the 4% **CPI** (**consumer price index** or commonly known as the inflation indicator). So, the 7.5% return is just a number (**nominal return**). The real actual growth in value is approximately 7.5%-4% (inflation) = 3.5%.

Problem 2: Management fees: Unfortunately for us Canadians, we don't have the same economies of scale nor the same competition between asset managers as our neighbors to the South, so we tend to have much higher MERs. According to Thompson Reuters, the average Canadian bond fund

MER is about 1.7%, leaving the average investor with a grand total of 1.8% (3.5% - 1.7%).

I forgot to mention, if you are holding this fund outside your RRSP or TFSA account, you will have to pay tax on your "gain".

As we have hinted at before, risk and reward are very closely related in the investment world. Bonds are not without risks however; there are quite a few risks to be taken into consideration when investing in bonds.

WHY WOULD YOU BUY A PUBLIC BOND?

There are few reasons to excuse individuals from buying an investment grade public bond or bond fund. The only real excuse is if you have been unfortunate in your ability to save for retirement and have been left in a position where running out of funds before running out of life is a large concern. No one deserves to make it to their golden years and worry about exhausting their funds before they pass away.

Another, almost excusable situation is when someone honestly can't emotionally bear the ups and downs of the market. Investing can be an anxiety inducing endeavor. However, after reading this book you may feel much better prepared to face the financial challenge ahead. The easiest way to dispel investment anxiety is to educate yourself and plan. If you are reading this book at a young age, good for you; time is on your side! You may want to look harder for ways to gain control of your financial plan, and that may include looking outside the plain vanilla public market.

Chapter 7
Begin with the End in Mind: Retirement

"If you don't know where you are going, you will wind up somewhere else."
- Yogi Berra

What I am about to explain in this chapter was in large part the main inspiration for this book. Ignorance will rob you of your wealth. Nowhere is this more true than in the world of investments.

Imagine the following scenario:

You are a money savvy 25 year old. Having started your first serious job a few years ago, through budgeting properly, you were able to save a nice chunk of money. You have saved an average of 20% of your income for the last 5 years, or $33 per day, which is $165 per week, roughly $8,000 per year, and about $40,000 in total. You have yet to start investing any of it, even though you have thought about it many times. So, not knowing where to look for investment advice, you do what most people would: walk into a bank/financial planners office.

ARE YOU READY FOR THIS?

After you walk through the door, you are likely to go through some sort of risk assessment and goals analysis. The advisor will poke and prod to find out how much money you need to retire and how long you intend to work. After all the questions, he will recommend a "diversified portfolio" of stocks and bonds based on your age, goals, and risk tolerance. I can almost guarantee that he will be promoting an actively managed mutual fund with a juicy MER. At this point, I would challenge you to ask the advisor if he can replicate the same strategy using low-fee ETFs. If the answer is "no," I would encourage you to consider why you are paying for his advice if you can replicate his plan at 1/10th the fee (I will detail the standard plan in chapter 11). I recommend that if you have any interest in getting ahead through your own learning, you should turn around and exit stage left. Why?

The mutual fund sales person (and I do mean that in every sense of the word) is going to recommend you buy a fund that is managed by some extremely intelligent people whom you will never meet. They will do you the favor of managing your money for the very 'low' cost of 2%-2.5% per year. The problem is, what you don't know will cost you, and your ignorance is their profit.

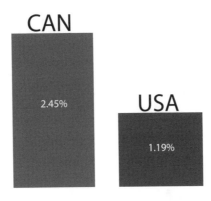

Average Active Equity Fund MERs

The average MER of U.S. mutual funds is about 1.19%, according to Vanguard, while Canada's equity funds are somewhere between 2.42% and 2.52%, according to Morningstar® Canada.

I'm going to say this as clearly as possible: do not pay this fee if you can avoid it. Nine times out of ten, the professional manager is not worth the fee they charge, and I can prove it to you here.

Take the $40,000 you have saved, and consider the following two options while planning your retirement at age 65.

A: An all equity mutual fund that invests in a diversified stock portfolio of professionally picked stocks.

B: An ETF, the electronic product that replicates the entire stock market.

Option A: The mutual fund does as it should, gaining the market rate of return in most years, netting you 10% per year before fees. After your 2% MER, this becomes 8% (we are not going to consider taxes or inflation in this example, but trust me, they only make things worse). After 40 years, $40,000 becomes approximately $867,000.

This exponential growth is brought about by what Albert Einstein called "the most powerful thing in the world," the miracle of compounding returns.

Option B: The ETF also does as it should, matching the market return exactly. It also returns the market rate of 10%, but because of the lack of a human manager, among other smaller considerations, the fee for such a product is approximately only 20 basis points or .2%, 1/10th the fees of the managed fund. So, your net return becomes 9.8%, and your resulting end value at retirement is $1,683,000.

Same product, with almost double the return; how can this be so? In a nutshell, the 2% fee not only takes your money directly out of your pocket, but it also prevents this money from compounding for many years into the future (which is the key point here). This "ghost fee" is called opportunity cost; it is the money you "would have made" if you didn't have to pay the management fee.

 It is important to note that 9/10ths of the return your portfolio will achieve is not determined by the manager you choose or the stocks they pick. Your returns from investing in a diversified portfolio will be determined primarily by the fact that you invested in the market itself: nothing more and nothing less. 85% of managers will not beat the market in a given year after their fees (MERs) are considered. That number jumps to over 99% of managers unable to beat the market when you monitor performance over a long period, say 20 years.

If you are interested in taking control of your plan using ETFs and the passive strategies they permit, consider visiting *Canadian Couch Potato.*[20] Dan Bortolotti does a fantastic job of cutting to the core of the issues. His plain spoken explanations expose the myth of active management and show the average Canadian how to approach retirement planning in a relaxed manner.

Investment managers are well aware of the performance challenges that they face individually and as a group. They know that any "diversified" portfolio of over 23 stocks or so, will almost never beat the market over a 5 year period. This is why in studies conducted by investment managers themselves, the most important determinant to client satisfaction was how much clients liked their broker. In every survey, the broker relationship ranked as most important. The importance of return in their portfolio ranked around number 4 on their priority list. I'm not sure why these people were investing if not to make money. If clients understood how to compare investment returns between managers or compare the managers to their benchmarks, these rankings would change. Returns would become the number one driver of client retention.

I'm not saying that a financial planner adds no value at all. Human psychology and history will show, that left to our own devices, humans make very emotionally driven, poor investment decisions. Even many experienced investors fall victim to their emotions. There-in lies the problem: <u>the key to investment performance in the public markets is not investment knowledge, but effective control of one's irrational human emotion</u>.

A good financial planner should educate you about suitable investment vehicles, opportunities, and products. Most importantly, they are there to design an investment plan and help you stick to it. If you understand the fees and determine they are fair, by all means choose any advisor you like.

If you want to go beyond the ordinary, you will have to self-educate. There are many resources available for someone looking to learn how to design their own financial plan. Each one of the books I recommend can serve this purpose. Taking ownership of your plan, while intimidating at first, can be extremely rewarding.

If you are going to pay someone to tell you how to invest, consider seeking out a fee only advisor. Fee only advisors are paid by their clients. This means that they do not take referral fees, kickbacks, or any other compensation, except what you pay them. The fee only advisor can give you access to many more products and will truly help you get the one that fits your needs. This means that you are going to get much different advice than from your local bank or Investco. Mutual fund sales people are paid by mutual funds. I'm sure you can easily identify the problem here; the mutual fund sales person is only going to be influenced to sell you what the mutual fund companies want him to sell you.

A financial planner/advisor primarily helps you to draw up an investment plan or **Investment Policy Statement (IPS)**. Such a plan indicates what you invest in (or your asset allocation between stocks and bonds) and when to change that mix. There are different schools of thought on this topic, but I will summarize two of the most popular ideas.

 # 1 Risk Reduction: This is by far the most popular of the two. As you get older, you can ill afford to have wild swings in your portfolio, so you must reduce your risk or exposure to stocks and increase your exposure to bonds as you age. One of the common rules of thumb here is that your exposure to stocks should equal 120 minus your age. So, a 20 year old would be 100% invested in stocks, and by age 100, they would have 20% exposure to "riskier" assets.

I would agree with this idea if one is at risk of outliving his assets or is in need of consistent income. If running out of money is a concern, I think it's best to play it safe. Hopefully, after reading this book, running out of money will be the least of your concerns, and your days will be spent pondering how you can best use your wealth as a tool for leaving the world a better place.

 # 2 Constant exposure: If running out of money is not a concern, why would you reduce your exposure to systematic risk? If you want to pass on as much wealth as possible to your heirs, keep the pedal to the metal, remaining fully invested in equities and other mediums, as they have a higher average return than bonds.

This topic can become extremely complex, and that is not the purpose of this book. If you are interested in the details of the academic proofs for what I am explaining here in this chapter, please check out the following books.

 Mark T. Hebner. *Index Funds: The 12-Step Recovery Program for Active Investors.* Mark explains in extreme detail, the reasons why passive investing outperforms. He recommends a passive strategy with a bias to small cap, value stocks.

John C. Bogle has written a great book on the subject of capturing as much of the market return as possible. He provides an in-depth analysis of the human element of investment decision making. It's called: *The Little Book of Common Sense Investing: The Only Way to Guarantee Your Fair Share of Stock Market Returns.* I recommend getting the audio book version.

Joel Greenblatt. *The Big Secret for the Small Investor: A New Route to Long-Term Investment Success.* Again, you may want to get the audio book and save this for a long road trip.

If you are interested in learning about the different schools of thought with regard to asset allocation please check out:

 Nick Murray. *Simple Wealth, Inevitable Wealth: How You and Your Financial Advisor Can Grow Your Fortune in Stock Mutual Funds.*

Finally, to tie it all together, I recommend:

Keith Matthews. *The Empowered Investor: A Guide to Building Better Portfolios.*

Chapter 8
Alternative Investments

"Traditional investment vehicles, such as IRAs, CDs, stocks and bonds, do have their place, but for the rich they are used more as temporary storage facilities rather than life-long homes." - Bo Bennett

I have frequently mentioned the option to invest outside the traditional financial markets as a way to supercharge your financial plan. I believe the stock market is one of many vehicles to get to financial freedom. From a diversification standpoint, it makes more sense to diversify between markets as well as within markets. These alternatives have the potential for very favorable returns, and this is where I personally invest most of my money.

Alternatives are not a new idea, this is how the big boys invest. For example, Yale University's endowment fund is the second largest in the world at $16 billion. During a 10 year period, when the S&P 500 returned -2.2%, this fund generated over 11.8% by diversifying outside the public markets. When their stocks didn't do very well, they had alternative investments to pick up the slack. As of 2010, they only had 17% of their investments in stocks and 4% in bonds; as of 2011, they had even less. Stocks and bonds are the two investments that the bank tells you to put all of your money into, because that is what the bank sells. If the smart money is able to diversify between markets, why shouldn't you? These alternative investments are becoming more accessible to Canadians every day.

This increased accessibility comes not a moment too soon, as many Canadians are finding their retirement plans severely underfunded. Their standard portfolio mix of stocks and bonds, with 2%+ management fees, is not going to get them where they need to go. The attractive investments in the private market may just be the solution for many of these people. In a recent popular survey by Fidelity Investments, it was found that 86% of today's millionaires considered themselves "self made," meaning they didn't make their money on the stock market. Let's take a look at some of the options out there and the opportunities they present.

REAL ESTATE

Real estate is a very popular alternative to the stock market and a personal favorite of mine. In the same survey by Fidelity Investments, among the remaining 14% that were already wealthy, the sandbox they preferred was real estate. I will tell you a little secret that may surprise you: more than 80% of millionaires made their money from investments in real estate. What makes real estate so appealing? Let's spend a bit of time on this.

CASH FLOW

The most important rule of thumb for investing in real estate is that you should always invest for positive cash flow; you should always buy an asset that puts money in your pocket after covering your monthly expenses. The value of real estate can fluctuate, but if you are cash flow positive, you will always be moving in the right direction. As I mentioned before, this is always my number one rule: seek passive income.

LEVERAGE

It is common to borrow 80% of the value of a house and pay the loan down over a term of 25 years. Try doing that with a mutual fund and the loan officer will laugh you out of the bank. Why is this so? The value of real estate does not typically change as much as the value of financial securities (stocks/bonds). With this more stable value, you can borrow more of the value of the asset. When you borrow money to purchase an investment, that is called financial **leverage**. Let's see how this leverage works in action:

"Give me a lever long enough and a fulcrum on which to place it, and I shall move the world"- Archimedes

SIMPLIFIED EXAMPLE

Steve has $10,000; he can choose between two investment options: mutual funds or real estate. He expects that in the next year, each will increase in value by 10%.

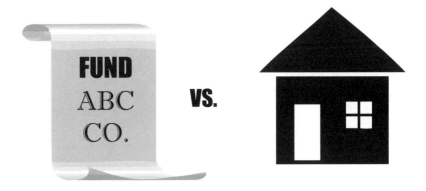

Scenario 1: Steve asks his bank to give him a loan to invest in a mutual fund. The bank rejects his loan application, and Steve invests his $10,000, sure that his investment will pay off.

Steve is right, and the mutual fund goes up 10% as he predicted. Steve now has $10,000 x 1.1 = $11,000.

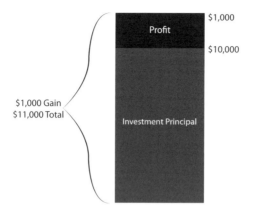

Scenario 2: Steve asks his bank to give him a loan to invest in a rental property. The bank accepts his application and loans him $90,000 to purchase a $100,000 house. Steve used his $10,000 as a down payment.

Steve purchases the property using the rents to pay the mortgage, insurance property taxes, fees, and maintenance. Again, Steve is correct, the value of the property increases by 10%. Steve now has a property worth $110,000. He decides to sell the property for $110,000. He pays the $90,000 loan back to the bank, and has $20,000 left.

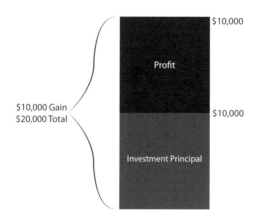

As you can see, investing in stocks yielded Steve $1,000, whereas investing in real estate netted him $10,000. The only difference was the amount of leverage he was allowed to apply.

When you take out a loan from the bank or any lending institution, their two main concerns are: what is the "security/collateral" of the loan, and how sure are they that the payments will be made. When you invest in something like a mutual fund, the payments from the fund on a monthly basis are small, and the value of the fund can change dramatically in one year. If you were to invest in an investment property, the value of the property is likely to remain more stable, and the rent from the property is also likely to be stable. Thus, banks are much more comfortable lending to investors to buy real estate, and many smart investors have taken advantage of this.

WHAT'S THE REAL RETURN?

From the example above, you can clearly see that without leverage, Steve earned only $1,000, and with leverage, he earned $10,000. It's necessary to understand the difference that financial leverage makes in changing an investor's **return on investment (ROI)**.

There is a very simple calculation to determine ROI: $[(Y_2-Y_1)/Y_1]$ x 100% or [(End Value - Beginning Value)/Beginning Value] x 100%

Scenario 1: No financial leverage [(11,000 - 10,000)/10, 000] x 100% = 10%

Scenario 2: Financial leverage [(20,000 - 10,000)/10,000] x 100% = 100%

Keep in mind, just as financial leverage can be your friend in positive years, it can be your enemy in negative years. Financial leverage will amplify the return both up and down.

This example of a single house investment is obviously simplified; real estate investment can be complex. However, it is achievable for almost everyone.

Real estate is sometimes called the "simple man's market." It just so happens that wealth creation doesn't need to be complicated.

U.S. REAL ESTATE

As of this writing, the U.S. economy is just beginning to pick itself up off the ground. Housing prices in some areas of America, are in some cases, as much as 70% off their peak values in 2007-2008. This has created a wave of investment into inexpensive U.S. real estate. This year so far, more than 90% of Phoenix real estate has been sold to Canadians. The entire state of Florida has seen international buyers swoop in and scoop up many deeply discounted deals.

In other areas of America, the rebound hasn't been as swift, and they are still floundering around the bottom of the market. This is a perfect example of the same market cycle moving at different paces in different areas. However, this was a much more severe broad decline than you would typically expect in a housing market. There are many reasons for this, but essentially, the main cause of the housing crash was the bubble created by the lack of lending regulation in 2002-2007. In one short year, the housing crash wiped out all the 2002-2007 gains and more.

When the dust settled after the crash, many investors, both foreign and domestic, started snapping up houses and apartment buildings like it was going out of style. I am lucky to be one of those investors; I currently own a portfolio of real estate in the South Eastern U.S. I get to enjoy passive cash-flow from our U.S. investments. What's more, we expect each property we purchase to more than double in value in less than 5 years.

EXEMPT MARKETS

We have discussed the public stock markets a lot. However, few people know that there is a completely separate market to buy shares in companies. There are some incredibly good deals offered in this market. This is the exempt market; here you can buy what are called **exempt market securities**. Typically, only wealthy Canadians accessed this market in the past, but it is becoming more mainstream for investors seeking higher returns, especially after the disappointing investment returns at the start of the 21st century.

The exempt markets do not provide bullet proof returns. Like any investment, there is always an element of risk. However, there is an argument to suggest that the risk/return relationship is more favorable in the exempt market. If you recall our discussion on risk, there are two main types: systematic (market) and unsystematic. Exempt markets do not bear systematic risk.

Exempt market securities are not subject to the "public opinion" of the market and therefore don't bear market risk. They bear only company specific risk; one less risk to consider. Let's take this one step further, and imagine a portfolio of 23 private market securities. Again, there is no "market index," and with diversification between investments, the investor remains free of systematic risk in the traditional sense. However, all investments in any market bear economic risk. If the economy does poorly, so will most businesses.

Considering the company specific risks exemplified by the Enron and WorldCom debacles in the public markets, combined with the market wide crashes in 2001 and 2008, I personally fail to see the great appeal of the public markets. The investors have no control over the results, and the results are not necessarily tied to the performance of the company in which they invested. Rather, performance is tied to market sentiment. That is to infer that other <u>people's opinion will determine the performance of your investment on a daily basis.</u> In the private/exempt market, the returns are based on the performance of the asset in which you invested.

Public vs Private Market Investments

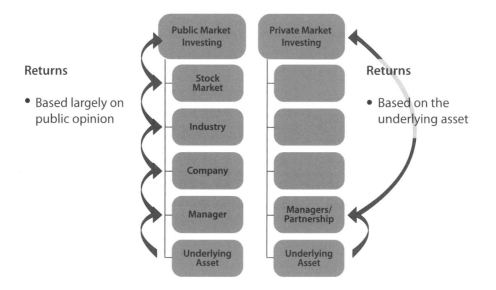

Returns

- Based largely on public opinion

Returns

- Based on the underlying asset

PRIVATE MARKETS BECOME MORE APPEALING TO CANADIANS

In 2009, this private market was redesigned with the introduction of new procedures and **oversight**. This has sent the money rushing in torrents over to the private markets. In fact, in 2011, the Canadian exempt market raised more new money than the public market. 2011 saw 142 billion dollars flood into exempt market securities.

Exempt market securities are so called because they are exempt from prospectus requirements (all publicly traded securities require a prospectus) and hence require less explanation than a prospectus (public) offering.

When selling shares in the private market, the sellers must ensure that they are selling to individuals who qualify to purchase the shares. Not every province has the same rules regarding who can buy these private shares. Depending in which province the shares are being sold, the investor may be qualified to buy the investment under an "exemption." Common exemptions include:

- Issue an **offering memorandum** in lieu of a prospectus, allowing anyone to invest up to a limit (not available in Ontario at this time)
- Sell to **accredited investors**
- Sell to **eligible investors**
- Sell to family, friends and close business associates
- Sell a minimum of $150,000 per transaction

I live in BC where there are no restrictions to worry about; Nova Scotia, New Brunswick, and Newfoundland also have the same advantage. Anyone over the age of 18 can invest any amount. The prairie provinces, PEI and Quebec, make this market fairly accessible, while Ontario remains the most restrictive market.

In this market, you gain direct access to the companies that have some of the best and most lucrative ideas. One of the benefits of having "direct access" is the lack of volatility in this market. These securities are not valued on a daily basis and are not subject to the ups and downs of the market. They will not be "dragged down" by a falling market, and there will be no roller coaster of emotions while you watch the value of your investment see-saw month after month. I like to think about it as having a "set it and forget it" mentality built in by design.

It should be noted that this lack of volatility comes from the lack of daily pricing. Most times, issuers of exempt securities are not interested in all the expenses and effort it takes to list on the public exchange. Either their business isn't big enough, or they don't want the obligations and costs of all the filings, reports, and audits involved with listing their stock on the public market. Exempt market securities may involve a "higher level" of risk, because of this lack of **continuous disclosure**.

There is no established secondary market for exempt market securities, meaning you can't simply decide to sell your shares any day. There are typically commitment periods of multiple years; once you have bought the investment, you must hold it to the end.

Let's not forget, private companies built the continent. In fact, nothing has changed, it's just not as easy to do because of the government requirements. Yes, the government has put these requirements in for the protection of the investor. However, there comes a point when you have to question the motivation behind the protection and the validity of the protection. While there is regulation in the private market, it isn't to the same level as the public markets, making it much easier (and less costly) to bring an investment opportunity to the market. There is no requirement for the management to continuously report to the investors on the status of the investment or produce ongoing reports that state changes in material facts. This is required in the public markets, therefore costing a lot of money in overhead to run a public company. Unfortunately, this overhead reduces the money flow back to the investor. Exempt market issuers do not face these sometimes overbearing requirements and as a result are much more agile and flexible, with the ability to move quickly to seize opportunity.

There is almost always a **lock up period** for these securities. This means that you must commit your funds to the investment for a certain number of years, sometimes 5-7 years. If you require access to all your funds at all times, then it's possible exempt securities are not your cup of tea. ETFs are well known for their **liquidity**, if you have to invest in the public market. I think that it's important to recognize that, while you can't access your funds for the lock up period, this may not be a terrible idea. Because of the lack of an active market for these shares, there is no opportunity to become fearful and sell at the wrong time. Equally important to note is that, many of these private market companies have stellar track records of success. Many of the companies listed on the private market have decades worth of solid performance history, displaying consistent ability to preserve capital, pay very attractive yields, remain tax efficient, and provide lots of capital gain opportunities.

Many of the opportunities in the private market are RRSP and TFSA eligible. Unless you are in your late 50's or older, you won't likely be taking your RRSP funds out anytime soon without facing serious tax penalties. So, the fact that you can't access your money shouldn't be of great concern.

Another benefit of exempt market securities is that they have a low **correlation** to the public markets. This means that it doesn't matter as much what is happening in the stock market, the private market won't really be affected. This "true diversification" is very important. Think about it; if diversification is such a good idea, doesn't it make sense to diversify between markets as well as within markets?

Yet another great feature of some exempt market opportunities is the ability to flow through the costs of the company to the investor. Why would you want to flow through a cost? The advantage here is that you can claim a tax deduction. For example, I can invest $100,000 into a flow through partnership and immediately receive a $50,000 tax credit. The expenses of the company become expenses for my investment, and I get a tax benefit. This is an extremely attractive opportunity for people in high tax brackets.

Typically, there are four different kinds of deals you will encounter in the exempt market:

1. <u>Tax Shelter</u>: As described above, attractive for the high income, high net worth individual because of the opportunity for tax reduction.
2. <u>The Yield Play</u>: Often times, these companies don't want to share their profits, they are happy to borrow your money at a high interest rate.
3. <u>The Capital Gain Play</u>: This one is straight forward; you are expected to put money in, and if the value of the project increases, you get more money back at the end.
4. <u>The Hybrid</u>: A combination of 2 and 3; there is an income component, as well as potential for participation in the back end gain.

Exempt market securities are sold by **exempt market dealers** (EMDs) or investment dealers. When purchasing exempt securities, the due diligence is ultimately up to the investor. I would say this is the primary risk of investing in the private market. You must feel comfortable that you understand the investment you are making and whom you are making it with. There have been cases in the past where the trust of the investor was abused and people lost money (not unlike the public markets). This is why it's important to only invest in the private market through a registered dealer. The dealer creates a "due diligence buffer" for the investor, because they are responsible for doing their own due diligence before approving the investment for their product shelf. To see what kind of deals are available from an exempt market dealer, consider searching *Google: exempt market dealers (your city)*.[21]

Remember, the more control/responsibility you have over your money, the more opportunity you will have. Where there is more knowledge there is more control, and if you have the ability to seize the opportunities, there is often more reward.

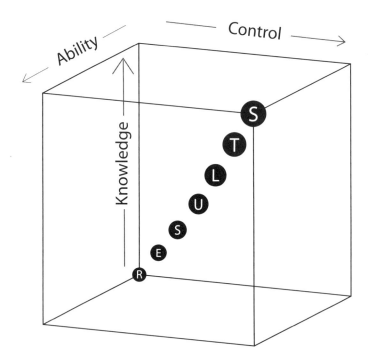

SMALL BUSINESS

As the world gets smaller and companies get larger, students are increasingly led to believe that they are in school to get a job, instead of to prepare for life. Unfortunately, this has more than a few adverse effects. One of those effects is that bright graduates are clamoring for a spot at the bottom. This pre-conditions them into being told what they can and can't do.

Falling in line with my proposal that risk, reward, and control are all positively related, small business ownership would be the pinnacle of this idea. Naturally, within the small business world, there are safer and riskier ventures. However, one thing is certain: the control belongs solely to the proprietor.

Small business ownership is an essential part of a healthy economy. Plainly said, the more people who own businesses, the more places there are to spend money and the more wealth is distributed throughout the system. This may be a bit difficult to grasp at first, but consider the following comparison.

AN ECONOMIC TALE OF TWO TOWNS

Imagine two towns. In Edgewater, everyone works at one of the town's big stores, Mall-Mart and Super-Shop. These stores are at the centre of town, and everyone drives from all over town to buy their goods at these stores. Most of the people in town also work at these stores, and therefore are dependent on the store for their survival. Because the average employee makes very little money working at one of the big stores, the only people who make a decent living in Edgewater are the managers of the stores. The well-paid managers live in Edgewater, but the very wealthy owners and investors live elsewhere. So, most of the money that is made in Edgewater is exported out of town to the pockets of the owners and spent in cities far away. This leaves little money in Edgewater.

Edgewater

In Bridgewater, the economy is completely different. There are no huge businesses that sell every foreign made product under the sun; there are only small local businesses. Because there are only small businesses, there are many business owners. These business owners make or build their own products and know their customers by name. Even better, the business owners live in Bridgewater! When they make money, they spend it at the other Bridgewater businesses. This keeps lots of money in Bridgewater, allowing the people of Bridgewater to develop their town by building parks, sidewalks, roads, and bridges. They invest in their schools and education, put on plays, and host music festivals in some of their many public parks. The money also enables the town to have better public programs, libraries, and recreation centers.

Bridgewater

If there are more places and opportunities to spend, money is recycled back into the same economy (in our case the town), and there is more wealth created. A dollar only creates value if it is spent. In Edgewater, there are only a couple of opportunities to spend the money. In Bridgewater, money shoots back and forth from business to business, and as a result, more things are sold and more wealth created.

Business owners are brave souls; they have what it takes to say, "I am the best person to determine what happens in my life, I am my own boss." No one else can say that, because everyone else has a boss. If you want to be the boss, you have to take the risk. If you can't figure out a way to solve the problems that come up, the problem will likely never be solved. That can be a huge challenge, but with it comes incredible reward.

These people are also wise enough to acknowledge that you can't know every single variable before making your move, or you will never move at all. I always recommend that you understand an investment before you put money in; business ownership is no different.

However, you need to understand the large components, and the details can be dealt with when the time comes. Successful people don't let all the nitty gritty details give them **analysis paralysis**. They move forward into the unknown, trusting that they will be able to handle what comes their way.

There are a ton of benefits to being a small business owner, not least of which are the tax benefits. Remember, the business gets to deduct its expenses before it pays its taxes. Conversely, an employee gets taxed before they get to spend. That is a massive advantage for the business. Also, a small business gets taxed at a lower, more favorable rate than an employee.

 As I mentioned before, everyone should own some sort of business, even if it were a little home based business or a multi-level marketing business. These little home based businesses cost pennies to run and pay pounds back in tax benefits. Who knows how many people will re-discover the feeling of empowerment, that was snatched away from them when they were told from day one in the classroom that they were supposed to get a job.

This healthy interaction is what is needed to keep wealth distributed in a healthy economy. If all that exists are large corporations that have control over how much people get paid, the economy will slip into the Edgewater example. Few people will control most of the money, and the majority of people will have very little. Small businesses are essential to keeping the economy strong, keeping communities responsive to their particular needs, and most of all, keeping the wealth in the hands of the many, not only the few.

PRIVATE EQUITY, VENTURE CAPITAL AND ANGEL INVESTING

In the world of finance and investing, private equity is a distinct asset class. It is different from typical public market securities, as private equity firms invest in companies that are not listed on the stock market.

Money for these private equity transactions come from private investors who place money in a fund designed for a specific purpose. A private equity investment will be made by a private equity firm, venture capital firm, or an angel investor. Each of these categories of investor has its own set of goals, preferences, and investment strategies. However, all provide capital to a company to promote expansion, product development, or restructuring of the company's operations, management, or ownership. There are many different strategies that are pursued by private equity funds. Some of them include: **leveraged buyouts**, growth capital, venture capital, and distressed/special situations. I encourage you to research these terms for more information.

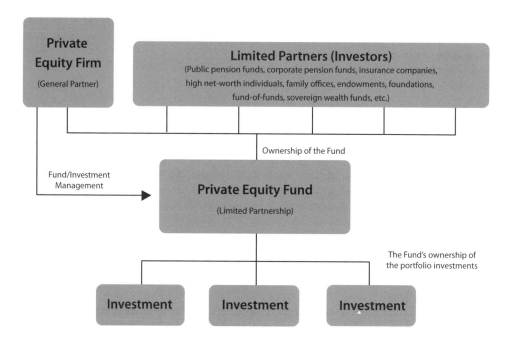

Generally, private equity firms deal only with individuals who are accredited investors. There are also typically lock up periods for these investors, 5-7 years is common. Fund managers are usually compensated by an **ad valorem fee**. For example, they may be paid 2% of the funds under management on an annual basis. They are also compensated by a performance incentive which is called the **carried interest**.

HEDGE FUNDS

Hedge funds are investment funds that can apply more complex investment strategies than typical mutual funds or ETFs. Also, they are generally available only to specific types of investors, such as pension funds, endowments, foundations, or high-net-worth individuals who are considered sophisticated.

Hedge funds usually invest in publicly traded companies, however they employ a very wide array of strategies, and make use of techniques, such as **short selling** and leverage.

Lock up periods are common, although not as restrictive as private equity funds. Management compensation for this type of fund is typically an ad valorem fee and an annual performance bonus based on return. For example, for returns above some **hurdle rate**, the manager receives 20% of the gain above this point onward. It's important to note the presence of a **high watermark** provision. This is a condition by which a manager has to create real growth in the portfolio before receiving his incentive bonus. Without this provision, the manager could simply remake the money he has already made after a drop fund value and be able to "double dip" on his incentive fee.

DERIVATIVES

A financial derivative is an investment vehicle that controls an underlying asset. For example, you can buy a derivative that controls 100 shares of a particular stock. These derivatives are varied in nature and extremely complex and volatile. When used correctly, they can be used to enhance return and even reduce risk. However, in the wrong hands, they can truly lead to disaster. I highly recommend that beginners stay away from trading in derivatives until they gain a complete understanding of how to use them.

It is possible to gain an understanding of derivatives trading using stock simulators, like the one I suggested on Investopedia. I was in university when I first started trading derivatives. I certainly wish I knew about those simulators back then! Like I always say, I received two educations at business school: one in the classroom and one in the market.

 If you want to learn how real investors invest their money, I suggest you read (or listen to) the following books by Robert Kiyosaki. He explains key differences between how rich and poor people invest. Hint- none of his money is in stocks, bonds, or mutual funds.

Robert Kiyosaki. *Unfair Advantage: The Power of Financial Education.*

Robert Kiyosaki. *Rich Dad's Guide to Investing: What the Rich Invest In, That the Poor and Middle Class Do Not!*

Chapter 9
Economics: What You Need To Know

"We have always known that heedless self-interest was bad morals; we now know that it is bad economics." - Franklin D. Roosevelt

In my opinion, economics should be as widely taught as history. I cannot fathom how pre-calculus trumps economics as a high school requirement. There are two basic fields of economics. First, there is micro-economics, which deals with small scale economics, such as pricing in a store or how competition between sellers drives down prices. There are many interesting topics that will educate you on how the business world works.

Macro-economics, macro meaning big, focuses on larger issues. Issues such as, what would be the effect on the economy if we spent more money on healthcare? Our discussion will centre more on macro economics.

I find macro economics incredibly useful when reading the newspaper. There are so many things in the newspaper that make so much more sense when you have a little knowledge of economics, such as: interest rate policy, tax policy, social issues like government spending, exports, imports, exchange rates, and the list goes on.

Here are a few key things you need to know about economics:

GROSS DOMESTIC PRODUCT (GDP)

GDP is probably the most important term to understand in economics. It is certainly the most commonly used term in the newspaper regarding the economy, and therefore it is very important for everyone to know and understand.

Definition: Gross Domestic Product = The monetary value of all officially recognized goods and services produced within a country's borders in a year.

Importance: The importance of GDP is that it is often used as a benchmark to measure how much "stuff" a country produced in a single year and how this compares to previous years. If GDP is increasing year to year, the country is believed to have grown. If GDP is shrinking year to year, the country's production has decreased.

At times, GDP is used as a measurement of productivity of a nation on a per person basis. Obviously, some large countries will have high GDPs compared to smaller countries, and so GDP can be measured "per capita" (per person). This indicates how much a country is producing for every citizen.

Although GDP is sometimes used as a proxy for a "quality of life" index, there are many different measurements that I think may do a better job at measuring that, such as the "gross national happiness" index.

CONSUMER PRICE INDEX (CPI)

This is a very important compliment to GDP, because it is essential in keeping perspective. Imagine if Canada's GDP was 100 in year 1. Next year, prices uniformly increase by 3%. If Canada produced the same amount of goods and services, the GDP would read 103 in year 2. The reason for this is not due to an increase in production, but rather an increase in prices.

Definition: CPI is the Consumer Price Index. This is the "price level": a measure of the average change over time in the prices paid by urban consumers for a market basket of consumer goods and services. Basically, there are a whole bunch of products (over 5,000) that are tracked, and when the average price of that basket of goods increases, you have an increase in the price level.

Importance: CPI is important for one main reason: inflation. You are going to read the word inflation umpteen times in your life, and you need to know what it really means. If the price index increases, that's inflation. In our example above, if GDP goes to 100 from 103, with no increase in production, that's an increase in prices only, not productivity. You may hear the term "real GDP" thrown around at times; this is a measurement of GDP with inflation taken out. This can be a very big problem for every Joe Soap out there working for a living. If the price of everything is going up, but you are making the same amount of money as the year before, you are effectively making less money.

For anyone who may have been in a labor union and has seen a certain minimum percentage increase in your wage, this is likely due to keep up with inflation. For people who invest in anything, you must be aware that even if your mutual funds returned 8.5% over 5 years, you didn't really gain 8.5% per year if inflation was at 4%; you only gained 4.5%. This becomes a huge problem for retirees and those on fixed dollar incomes or pensions (see the pension section). Inflation erodes the value of the dollars you do have.

EXCHANGE RATES

This is an important lesson to learn if you are going to do any international travel (highly recommended) or trade. An exchange rate is the price you have to pay for a currency.

Definition: The value of one currency in terms of another currency.

Importance: Exchange rates themselves are important to be aware of; if you are going to be traveling, buying, or selling anything in another country, you will want to make sure you know what your money is worth! You may also want to know something about how the rate is determined.

If you want to buy something from a foreign country, you have to buy the money before you can buy the products. If there is a large demand for the products in a country, it will drive up the demand for the currency, causing a higher exchange rate.

The dynamics of foreign exchange rates are always a difficult and daunting subject to master. There are many complex formulas and theories that accompany the subject. If there is one thing you should remember about exchange rates, it should be: first you buy the money, then you buy the goods. The currency will be worth what the world is willing to pay for it.

INTEREST RATES

Always an exciting topic, interest rates determine so much in our lives, and most people don't even realize it. Once you take out your first loan however, whether it be a car loan, a student loan, or a home loan, this very important subject will find new importance in your life.

Definition: An interest rate is simply the cost of money.

Importance: The key interest rate is set by the Director of the Bank of Canada. All other interest rates are bench marked off this rate. This means that one decision pretty much determines how much everyone has to pay for everything. This bears an especially large impact on business.

Think about it this way, you are going to start a business and you need to borrow $100,000. If the interest rate is 1%, in order to cover your interest payment for the year, you will have to have made at least $1,000 in profit. This doesn't seem like a very high hurdle. However, let's assume the interest rate is 10%, your minimum operating profit must now be $10,000. In the early 1980's, the prime rate was more than 20% in Canada and the USA. Can you imagine going to the bank and having to pay 20% on your loan to start a business or to buy a house?

As you can imagine, there weren't many new businesses started in the early 80's, nor were there many homes bought. In fact, with such expensive money, businesses and borrowers of all types suffered quite badly.

Now you may be asking yourself, "Why does the rate have to change at all?" That would be a fantastic question. The reason the rate changes, is to speed up or slow down the economy as business ebbs and flows through the business cycle. However, the primary reason the rate "should" change is to curb inflation, and only to curb inflation. Remember, inflation can be a killer for savings and earning power and the value of your money. Using interest rates to make money "expensive" when things are inflating irrationally, helps to keep order so that people can anticipate their needs in the future.

HIGH INTEREST RATES: A KILLER FOR BUSINESS

One problem that all businesses face is the chance of going **bankrupt**. All businesses either make and sell a product, or provide a service. They all make money, but many times they don't know exactly how much they are going to make. This means that their income is **variable**.

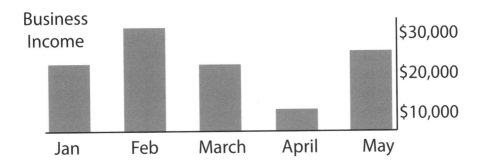

If the business has no expenses, the amount of money the business makes won't matter as much, and it can remain in business. However, once it has some fixed expenses, there is always a risk that the business could run out of money. Let's suppose the business took out a loan; that loan payment must be made whether money is made or not. If the interest on that loan is low, it's easier to "clear the hurdle" and make the required money.

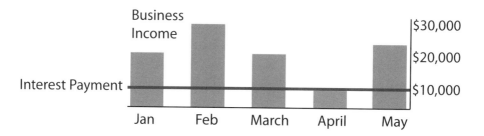

Let's suppose interest rates rise, the business will start struggling to make their payments. In a high interest rate environment, it's harder for businesses to make a profit. This is why there aren't as many businesses created, and less economic activity occurs when interest rates are high.

Chapter 10
Pensions, Insurance and Estate Planning

"'In this world, nothing can be said to be certain, except death and taxes."
- Benjamin Franklin

YOUR PENSION AND YOU: A COMPLEX RELATIONSHIP

I started this book commenting on how simple retirement planning was a few generations ago. Back in the good old days, an employee would be loyal to a company, and the company would repay that loyalty by taking care of the employee when they became too old to work.

The type of pension plan that I am describing is called a defined benefit pension plan. This is not to be confused with a defined contribution pension plan. Knowing the difference between the two could mean the difference between a happy, well funded retirement and a retirement filled with financial worry.

Defined benefit pension plans are what we all imagine a pension plan should be. It's a program where employees sacrifice some of their pay, that portion of pay is pooled and invested with each other and the company contributions. A manager is appointed by the company to manage the pension fund, and the proceeds of the fund go to ensure the standard of living of the employees in retirement. Often times, defined benefit plans take a few years to become "fully vested," meaning that an employee would need to have worked for the company for a certain period of time, before they could access the full benefit of the plan. Usually, there is a measurement by which the "benefit" is defined; for example, the company could pay at retirement 75% of the income level of the employee (indexed for inflation), for the average of the five highest earning years of employment.

A defined benefit means that the employee will receive a benefit, regardless of the cost of that benefit to the company. What this means essentially, is that the company is responsible to ensure the money is available to pay the obligations. This is extremely important to understand. Remember, the employee is responsible for contributing their portion of pay; the company is responsible for investing that money. The company must ensure that there is enough money at the end of the working life to support that individual. If the contributions are poorly invested, or there is a short fall caused by investment underperformance, the company is responsible to contribute from its retained earnings/profits to compensate for this shortcoming.

Contrast this with a defined contribution pension plan. A defined contribution pension plan is similar to a defined benefit plan, in that the employee is required to part with a portion of their paycheck in order to save for retirement. However, the responsibility is not on the company to ensure the sound investment of that money, nor is the company responsible for contributing any funds in a shortfall. Essentially, the employee is left largely to their own devices in making the investment decisions and in many cases fall victim to the plethora of pitfalls described in this book. To make matters worse, the employees are sometimes restricted in the range of investments they can make and through whom.

 I'm sure it comes as no surprise that many companies, with and without unions, are transforming their defined benefit plans to defined contribution plans as fast as they possibly can. In today's employment environment, when company loyalty and job security are decreasing rapidly, it's more important than ever before to understand and take responsibility for one's own financial education. You will likely be making the majority of your pension decisions; please do not take these decisions lightly, as they will be some of the most important financial decisions you will ever make.

INSURANCE

I have always been intrigued by the decisions that human beings make when it comes to risk. I will give you an example; I travel to the United States a lot, where in some states, there is no law requiring motorcyclists to wear helmets. I'm not an expert on motorcycle safety, but I am a motorcyclist, and what's more, I have survived three motorcycle accidents with little more than a scratch. When I am in Miami and I see a young 20-something man whip by me at 100mph wearing nothing but a T-shirt and a girlfriend on the back wearing nothing but a bikini, I shake my head like I just saw a mermaid riding a unicycle.

It's amazing to me how the human decision making process changes as we age. We tend to be much more reckless in our younger years. I haven't quoted my father yet in this book, but here I can't avoid it. As a father to 5 sons, he always told us to only "take calculated risks." He wasn't going to pretend that we weren't going to take risks; as young men we all did, but we heeded his advice.

In my observation, people often take the minimum level of precaution legally necessary. Let me explain; I would bet, that if tomorrow, seat belts were to become optional, many of us would rapidly stop using them. I would also bet that of those who chose not to use them, young people would be the majority. Why? Because young people like to think that they are invincible and nothing will happen to them.

Your life is not something that you should take lightly, and yes, I do recommend both seat belts and full safety gear on a motorcycle, but that's not the point here. My point is that what these young people may not realize, is the hole they will leave in the lives of their loved ones if something should happen to them.

I know it's disturbing to think about, but people die, and young people are more at risk for long term disability than death. Just as you should have an emergency fund if something should happen to your health or your income, you should have insurance for unexpected crises.

I'm not saying that every teenager should run out and get life insurance. What I am saying is that as you get older and take on financial responsibilities, get married and have children, there will be people dependent on your income for survival. You need to prepare for that situation if you are not already in it. What would happen if one day you weren't there?

In my opinion, life insurance and long-term disability should be compulsory, as is employment insurance and CPP. Interestingly, almost every labor union has a life insurance component integrated into their labor agreement. The reason for this is simple: people die and the workers know that. In the old days before life insurance, when a worker died, a hat was passed around, and hopefully some of the workers took care of the widow and children. Luckily, today we have more robust systems in place, and although nothing can replace a loved one, having proper insurance for an unexpected event relieves so much of the stress. No one is going to make you go out and get life and/or disability insurance, just like no one is going to make motorcyclists in some states wear helmets; just because it's not the law doesn't mean you shouldn't be proactive about your own safety.

 The only thing more certain than your retirement is your death! Life and long-term disability insurance is meant to replace your income for those who depend on you to survive. If you don't have any dependents yet, you may not need it. If you do have people who depend on you, then you better get yourself some insurance!

TERM VS WHOLE LIFE INSURANCE

There are two main types of life insurance: term and whole. Term life insurance covers you for a "term" or a set period of time. During that period of time, your payments (or premiums) are known and are generally the same amount each month. After that period, you have to renew, and your rate will change upward by a significant amount. If you die while covered, your beneficiaries will receive the payment of the value of your insurance policy, tax free; terms usually last about 20-25 years. In many ways, this works exactly like car insurance.

Whole life insurance covers you for just that, your whole life. Whole life premiums are much more expensive. There are two reasons for this; first, as you age, there is a higher chance that you will pass away. Assuming you paid the premiums until your death, you are going to pass away while covered by the insurance, meaning that sooner or later, the insurance company will have to pay out. Second, a whole life insurance plan usually includes the ability to "cash out" at some point in the future. What this means is that if you want to stop paying the premiums and give up the insurance, you can receive the cash value of your plan. Unfortunately, this cash value is much less than the premiums you have paid to date. The cash value feature works somewhat like a forced savings plan that gains interest at a low rate.

You are probably wondering which type of plan makes more sense. I can tell you that in my opinion, the term life makes more sense to most people who want to take control of their financial futures. I see it this way, because when you compare the two types of insurance, you face a very simple comparison: higher payments and longer coverage versus lower payments and shorter coverage. This is a pure financial question; the only two unknown factors are the cash value of the plan, which we will deal with shortly, and when you will die.

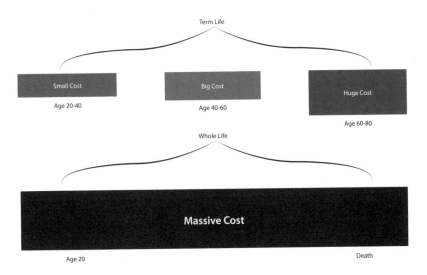

As you can see, it is much cheaper to opt for a term plan with the same amount of coverage. If you were to die at anytime in the first 20 years, you will be glad you went with the term plan. Well, you would be dead, but your family would benefit from it, as you would have saved them so much money in premiums!

When the second term comes along and you find yourself paying much more in premiums, the first thing you should do is thank your lucky stars that you are still alive. Next, regarding those payments, they will likely still be less expensive than whole life payments, provided you are still in good health.

Finally, the third term; assuming the first term was bought sometime in your 20's, you will be in your 60's by the time the third term rolls around. Again, thankfully, you are still alive and well. Term payments again are raised, and by a lot. However, let's not forget that the primary reason you were buying insurance was to replace your income should you pass unexpectedly. By the time you are in your 60's, you are going to start planning much more seriously for your transition to the next life. My point is, you won't necessarily be as concerned about replacing your income, because most of your income would have already been earned. If you make it to your 60's and look back at all the savings you had, you will be glad you had the opportunity to do something with the money you didn't pay in premiums. Keep in mind, all these years, you should have been investing the excess savings.

You may be wondering about the cash-value component. Here is the problem with cash-value; it's much less than you think, because you don't get all those premiums back. A large chunk of that money was being put aside for when you died. However, the much smaller 'savings' portion of it was squirreled away and locked into a nice safe investment for you, and the rate of return on that money is very low.

Let's pretend you could have afforded that whole life plan; should you do it? If you were to compare all the money that you saved versus the cash-value, the cash-value would be more; however what if you had been investing it the whole time? If you had paid a term life premium and invested the difference, the annual return "hurdle" you would have to beat would be somewhere around 5%-7%. After everything you have learned and everything you will learn about investments, I do hope you think you can do better than that.

This is not to say that whole life insurance is always a bad idea; wealthy people can use whole life in their estate planning by setting up an insurance trust that will pay their estate taxes from the proceeds of the policy, tax-free. For the growing number of people in their late 40's or early 50's who are just starting families, whole life is at least worth a look.

ESTATE PLANNING

Families with many assets are often focused on the secure and tax efficient transfer of wealth to the next generation. Naturally, this makes sense as you would need to have assets to be able to pass them on. Estate planning is not a "hot topic", but like insurance, it's something that needs to be addressed, as failure to do so could be very costly. You should ask yourself, if today was my last day, would anyone know what my wishes were and how they are to be carried out? If not, you may want to consider forming a plan to transfer your estate to your loved ones when you pass.

Regardless of your income and the value of your assets, everyone should have a will, if for no other reason than for convenience sake. You don't want to put your loved ones in a position to have to sort out the logistics of dividing your assets should you die "intestate," meaning without a will. Depending on your age and the age of your heirs, you may even consider transferring some assets before your death.

 Wealth transfer and estate planning are definitely some of the more tedious and cumbersome duties of an investor. While it can be quite difficult to wrap your head around all the details, I can recommend a book that may help you. The title of the book is: *The Cottage, the Spider Brooch, and the Second Wife* by Sandy Cardy. This book integrates the common ins and outs of estate planning into a story line, which makes it palatable for the average reader.

Few people take the time to learn the ins and outs of how to make their "final tax return" as efficient as possible. Given the complexities of the issue and what is at stake, versus the cost of professional help, I recommend seeking out a competent estate planner. The book I recommended will simply allow you to gain an appreciation for the complexities of the issue and allow you to speak to your advisor without being immediately bamboozled.

Chapter 11
Putting It All Together

"Two roads diverged in a wood, and I took the one less traveled by, and that has made all the difference." - Robert Frost

Up to this point, we have reviewed the standard talking points of most beginner's books in financial planning, and we have gone past that basic body of knowledge to explore some additional relevant areas of personal finance. What I haven't done to this point is given you a plan to follow. Many people write books that push the reader to develop a financial plan, tailored and managed by a mutual fund sales person. My premise at the beginning of this book is that this simply raises you to a higher level of financial slavery. If the best you can do is walk in the door of your financial planners office, throw your hands up, bury your head, and allow him to go to work, you will end up doing the same thing that most other people do and garner the same result.

I believe that if you are reading this book, it is to improve on the 'average' result. To do better than the average, you are going to have to do something yourself. You will have to make some decisions, and you are going to have to make assessments for yourself. You will have to take yourself out of the average situation at your local bank or financial planners office, and start looking harder for less ubiquitous opportunities.

To understand what "different" looks like, I will show you what "average" looks like first. The assumption for this projection is that each asset class performs at its historical average: $40,000 initial contribution and $5,000 annual contributions from age 30 - 65. The MER is assumed to be 2.25% for mutual funds.

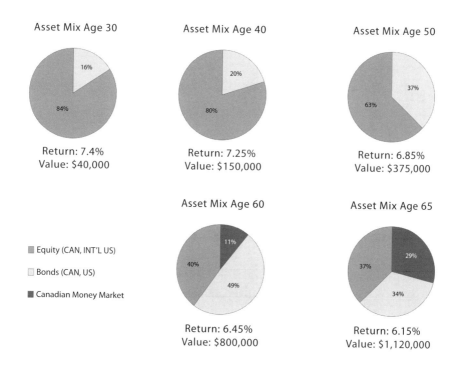

This is a typical path projected by your average financial planner; almost every plan will follow the same pattern. This one is designed for someone age 30 and planning to retire at age 65. Notice how this plan starts with 85% equity/stock exposure and slowly reduces "risk" by blending in more bonds as you age. *Fidelity's investment planning tool[22]* is useful in displaying this standard path.

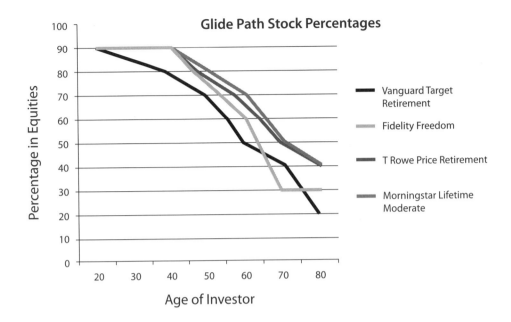

 In his book, *Index Funds* and on his website *IFA.com*,[23] Marc Hebner lays out a simple and beautiful plan that follows a logical dial down of risk. It is artfully displayed in his material, and I highly suggest you check out his *sequence of portfolios*[24] that glide along as one ages. This is a masterful execution of a typical plan, and the use of index funds is the genius in this plan. Using the low cost option to execute a similar plan, the investor keeps more of the gains compared to actively managed portfolios.

Here is a projection of a plan using the low cost indexing products: same $40,000 initial contribution, same $5,000 contribution, same investment horizon, but with a 1% MER.

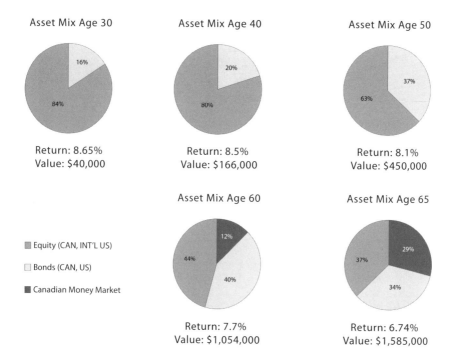

Asset Mix Age 30
Return: 8.65%
Value: $40,000

Asset Mix Age 40
Return: 8.5%
Value: $166,000

Asset Mix Age 50
Return: 8.1%
Value: $450,000

■ Equity (CAN, INT'L US)
☐ Bonds (CAN, US)
■ Canadian Money Market

Asset Mix Age 60
Return: 7.7%
Value: $1,054,000

Asset Mix Age 65
Return: 6.74%
Value: $1,585,000

We have looked at bonds and their ability to generate real wealth. One of the effects of increasing bond exposure over the life of the plan is to tamp down on variability of return, or specifically losses. This will keep the plan value more stable. With 100% equity exposure throughout, the plan will maintain a similar risk level. There are many who would argue that a plan should become more conservative over time. I don't disagree, IF that person faces a real chance that they could outlive their assets, they should plan for this accordingly. However, if someone plans prudently, especially from a young age, or has sufficient assets where outliving their funds isn't an issue, they should reconsider the need to reduce risk as they age. Reducing risk will reduce returns as well.

Next let's look at what the same plan would look like with 100% equity exposure and no fees throughout the entire investment horizon. This displays a periodic "loss to fees, bonds, and opportunity cost" comparison between the plans.

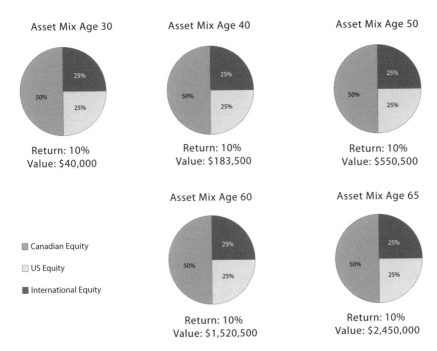

The only asset class represented in this investment plan is public equities. As I have described, <u>there are so many options outside the world of publicly traded stocks, and the returns in these alternative markets are arguably more attractive.</u> Just think, if the only market promoted is the stock market, what do you think is going to happen? Aside from becoming very populated with investors and very efficient as a result, it will become very hard to make money, because everyone is doing it. This may offer some sort of security for people, knowing that everyone is in the same boat. However, given the performance of this market over the last decade and the two stock market crashes during that time, I don't see how someone can view this as a "safe" way to go.

Personally, the stock market is a very small part of my investment portfolio. I suggest that stock market investment should be limited to only your investments which you would like to remain liquid in the short term. Even with your RRSP or TFSA money, there are other options besides actively managed mutual funds.

If you are going to step into control of your investments, you will need to start understanding how to build an investment plan for yourself. Luckily, the *Ontario Government*[25] has provided a wonderful resource to help you with just that.

OTHER OPTIONS

One of the easiest options in addition to ETFs (instead of active funds) for registered/retirement money, would be to invest in exempt or "private" market securities.

Exempt securities do not have a secondary market. This means, it's not a stock exchange where you see the price change daily. There is usually no option to sell, it truly is the embodiment of Warren Buffett's "punch card" investment mentality. You buy, you hold, you prosper. As Buffett has indicated on many occasions, when he finds an investment he likes, his holding period is forever. The holding period for exempt market securities isn't forever, but it is true that you will usually not be able to sell your investment in the interim. You will be required to hold it until the investment term as stated in the offering documents has passed.

You can access exempt/private market securities by searching for a dealing representative of a registered exempt market dealer operating in your area. There are many exempt market dealers in Canada. Although they are not as common as mutual fund dealers, they are gaining popularity, because people are starting to seek better and more consistent returns. *Google: exempt market dealers (your city)*[26] to see examples of exempt products.

Another option is to invest directly in real estate by purchasing property yourself. You will not be able to do this easily with money from your RRSP or TFSA. If you are able to spare the cash/credit to invest in real estate, it is a fantastic vehicle: one of my personal favorites and a favorite of many wealthy people.

Alternatively, you can invest in real estate through a REIT or real estate fund, with RRSP/TFSA money. This stands for Real Estate Investment Trust; they can be both private and public. This vehicle allows you to own units in a pooled investment portfolio of many properties. Keep in mind that the more passive you are, the lower your return is likely to be.

Small business is always an option for people with some money to invest. In my opinion, the best small business to invest in is always your own. I believe everyone should run some sort of business; I think it's healthy for the economy, and given the tax breaks, the decision to start your own business should be a no-brainer.

WHAT MY INVESTMENT PLAN LOOKS LIKE

Instead of simply accessing the normal route that leads to a financial advisor, people are starting to hunt for alternatives. The evolution has already begun; people have started to move away from actively managed funds and are moving toward discount brokerages, or attempting to do it themselves. With the emergence of the exempt markets, investors are starting to gain access to opportunities previously reserved for only the very wealthy. With a growing understanding of the tax advantages in real estate investing and small business, these areas are seeing much more activity from the savvy investor. This investor isn't the typical wealthy person throwing money at any opportunity in a suit, but a learned, self-educated, average person, who demands an above average result.

While I started investing in my teens, my path wasn't the model of stability as I stumbled my way through figuring it all out. I had to learn as I took my knocks, but through it all, I have learned about myself and my risk tolerance. Most importantly, I have learned what it's like to make mistakes. I can empathize with others who have made mistakes and caution those who are about to. If I could retroactively re-design my plan from scratch, it would look something like the following.

Let's assume the above average result is to start at age 20, with $10,000. Imagine the investment grows at approximately 15% per year with annual $7,000 contributions, re-investing all returns; this could be a possible scenario.

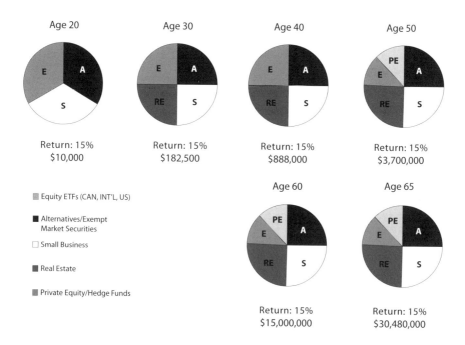

I'm not sure about you, but considering all the examples of financial plans, I like this one the best. At the time of this writing, I seem to be right on track, despite taking a lengthy detour through the derivatives world in my 20's.

It's been said in many different ways, that life will give you what you demand of it. I think that's true, and especially true when it comes to finance and investments. If you don't demand better for yourself, you will end up settling for the same result as the average Joe. I'm not sure if you noticed, but what the average Joe has been getting lately seems to be shrinking every year. It's up to you to demand more for yourself and shoulder the responsibility that comes with doing so. That will most definitely mean a life long journey of continuously developing your financial literacy and education. It may not be your passion, but if you are passionate about achieving your financial goals, maybe you can develop a tolerance to get you on your way to success. Starting is the hardest part, and that's why I wrote this book: to get you started.

Chapter 12
General Wisdom

"All that's necessary for the forces of evil to win in the world is for enough good men to do nothing." - Edmund Burke

LIVING WITH A CRITICAL EYE

All through high school, I was told that I was being trained to be a critical thinker. I am extremely lucky that through social media, my high school peers are largely still in contact with each other. I often think back to my days spent with them in the classroom and wonder how well we all learned to be critical and independent thinkers. In all honesty, I don't think we as a group learned that lesson very well. We were always told we should be critical and independent, but we were not shown how. We were told to question the world around us, but we were told not to question the authority of anyone at the private school we attended. I remember being voted "the most likely person to start a revolution." Needless to say, I pride myself on not being satisfied with the status quo.

Living life in this complicated world seems to require multiple advanced degrees. I'm not recommending that everyone go to university and study finance, I'm just recommending that people take ownership of their lives to learn about important subjects like health and wealth. If you learn just an ounce of information, it will save pounds of financial pain. One of my mentors once told me that he didn't care what his children did, as long as they enjoyed it; but he hoped, they would first learn to put themselves in a position to be able to choose what they loved, instead of forced to accept what they would grow to hate. What he meant by this is that, he wanted them to learn to be wise with their money first, become financially free, allowing them to really have time to do what they loved, whether it made a lot of money or not.

THE PSYCHOLOGY OF PERSONAL FINANCE: PSYCHOLOGICAL DEBT LEVELS

The Pareto Principle or 80/20 rule tells us that we as humans are separated in the way we think, and as a result, in the way we act. The rule states that, for many events or situations, roughly 80% of the effects come from 20% of the causes; for example, 80% of sales come from 20% of sales people.

Applying this idea to wealth, we see many people who face very dire financial situations; yet, some of them are able to rise up, even out of severe poverty, and seize financial freedom. What is it that allows them to find what it takes to refuse to accept the status quo? Personally, I think there is something inside them that remains restless until they achieve their goal. Psychologically, they are not able to handle being in their current financial situation, which is usually mired in debt.

Most people find it too difficult to work hard enough to change their situations when they get in a deep enough jam, especially if that deep jam is a financial one. Most people aren't able to pursue their dreams and their heart's desire, because they have become too psychologically comfortable with carrying the debt load they have.

There is a theory, that if you level the distribution of wealth amongst all people in America today and make everyone equal in assets, the wealth would find its way back to more or less its current place in approximately three years. Most people have what I call a "psychological debt level." This is the level of debt that they are comfortable carrying. This debt level isn't usually a dollar amount or absolute value, but a ratio or percentage of income. Given the average person's propensity to immediate gratification, this debt may likely be replenished by habit alone. I don't write this as a justification for things being the way they are; I write this so that people can acknowledge this, take ownership of it and look deep into their own behavior and the reasons for it.

For example, our friend Steve makes $48,000 per year, and he is comfortable having a $12,000 debt via lines of credit and credit cards. If he were to get a huge raise, increasing his salary to $96,000, he would reward himself handsomely and raise his debt level to $24,000 in lock-step with his rising income.

The problems with this are many, but none more so than what I call the "standard of living trap." Psychologically, it's very easy to move from an income level of $48,000/year to $96,000/year. However, it's much more difficult to move in the reverse. Given the level of job security these days, it's more and more likely that young people will see their income levels vary significantly in the first decade of work experience, and not always in a progressively upward manner. That wouldn't be a large problem if people could raise and lower their standard of living with their income. However, going from driving a Benz to riding the bus, going out to dinner to cooking at home, and losing your 'life of luxury' is extremely difficult for some. The attempt to live beyond their means is what often raises the 'psychological debt level' to a higher level, and unfortunately, it can often stay at that higher level. I'm not opposed to debt, I'm just opposed to bad debt. I hope by understanding what is likely to come, young people and not so young people can recognize these patterns and change them.

THE ACCELERATION OF MARKET CYCLES

I love studying the psychology of stock market investing. I love statistics, stocks, and technical analysis. Technical analysis is the practice of using charts to make investment decisions.

This is dismissed by some as a bunch of useless mumbo jumbo. However, in short term analysis, technicals have their place. The reason being, I see technical analysis as the graphical manifestation of investor psychology.

I encourage you to google "technical analysis", if you want to understand how people invest using graphs.

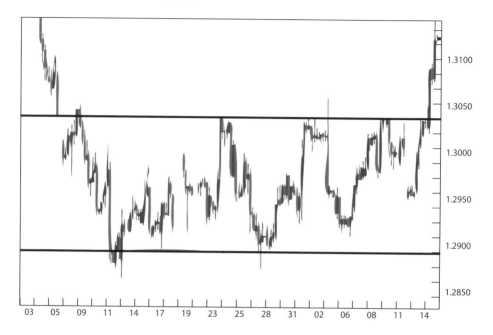

Warren Buffett said it best: In the long-term, the market is a weighing machine, in the short-term, it is a voting machine. What this means is that, in the long term, people weigh the facts and invest in companies based on reason. In the short term, the market is driven primarily by human emotion; those two emotions are mainly fear and greed. I have a theory, that despite how smart we humans think we are, the old adage will always remain true: fear and greed drive the market. The market will soar, and the market will crash. The only thing that will change as we advance into the future, is the frequency and severity with which our human emotions will repeat themselves. With the arrival of new technology, this frequency will likely increase at an increasing rate.

Have you ever heard of the "flash crash"? One day, in May 2010, the entire stock market experienced a 1,000 point crash and recovery in a single day. Look it up, it's quite something.

On the surface, most people would look back at history and scoff at the ignorance of the people in the early days of the stock market. They marvel at how naive people were allowing their wealth to disappear, buying high and selling low. However, nothing has changed; people still make decisions based on emotion. It's in our nature to do so. As long as that continues, technology will simply allow us to make the same mistakes repeatedly with increasing frequency and severity. That's why the 2008 and the 2010 crashes were so pronounced.

Have you ever eaten too much or had too much to drink? Have you ever told yourself in the midst of your suffering that you would never do that to yourself again? Was it truly the last time? The psychology and emotions of people of the past and present are no different. As long as people drive markets, those markets will more or less follow the same pattern of human behavior: a slow build up to a frenzied peak, then a sharp and swift downward over correction, and then a repeat. The trick is not to get caught up in the frenzy, and to have the good sense to buy when everyone is fearful. This applies not only to the stock market, but to every market and every investment opportunity. The sooner you are able to recognize the pattern and patiently take advantage of it, the sooner you will be vaulted ahead financially.

 Never underestimate how difficult this is to do. The trick is to be able to detach your emotions from your decision. However, I would like to give you a piece of advice for any passive investment: one of the most important things to be aware of when you have made a passive investment is not to watch it everyday. You will get a great indication of your future success by how little you follow your first equity investment. That seductive call of the trading software, begging you to trade is a siren's song. If you do not get on the emotional roller coaster, it allows you to make decisions in a logical manner.

THE PLIGHT OF THE MONEY MANAGER

Having started off wanting to be an investment advisor, I took to studying these individuals very closely. Through my work experiences, I was able to get a good idea of the money manager's mind-set.

I came to realize that many of them did not truly understand that they were destined to perform below average on their investment performance, especially after fees. Many didn't actually realize that they were not adding any value to the return in their clients' portfolios. Even worse, some of them did understand this, but didn't care.

The attitude of many brokers and advisors can be summed up in an encounter I had with one individual. He pulled me aside one day to make sure I understood the most important rule of managing money for other people. He said to me: "Son, you have to remember the golden rule, it isn't don't lose money for people, it's make sure to keep managing the money."

This person was paid not by commission but as a percentage of the assets he managed, ad valorem (like most high level investment advisors). What he was getting at was, it didn't matter to him if the client made money or lost money, because he was paid his annual fee regardless. As long as he was still in charge of managing the money, he was happy, and that's all that mattered. Most retail financial advisors are paid on both commissions and trailers.

I mentioned studies showing "client experience" to be the most important factor in client decision making, regarding whether to keep a money manager or move on. Portfolio performance often ranked below the top three. I feel this is the case, because often times clients lack the ability to accurately judge their money manager's performance and most importantly, the impact of their fees.

Luckily, this trend is starting to change. It's changing because many people have had a heck of a time watching their actively managed mutual funds or even their "tailor made" portfolios go nowhere with the stock market. In the "lost decade", clients not only lost money, but they lost because of management fees. In this situation, it was fairly easy to determine that the market was flat, but they were still charged high fees. This poor market performance combined with increased competition from low fee funds, discount brokerages, and low fee ETFs, has started to change the competitive landscape in Canadian money management.

The spirit of this book is to empower the reader to demand better for themselves. I feel people should do much more to educate themselves on how to make better financial decisions. There is a lot of information out there and many vehicles, products, and opportunities to invest. There is a lot of information, and it can be overwhelming; I get that. I do recognize that empowerment will be a long and inefficient process; not everyone can or has the desire to tailor their own investment plan.

There are cases where money managers are needed to care for those genuinely in need of their help. I'm not talking about the capable 20-something who's too lazy to learn how to manage his money. I'm talking about the disabled, the elderly, and people of that ilk. In these circumstances, money managers take on a role of an investment administrator with limited decision making capabilities, presuming there isn't an excessive amount of wealth involved.

Another scenario where money managers are useful is for the very wealthy. Having a lot of money can be a heck of a problem. Accountants, lawyers, estate planners, financial advisors, (not to mention all the people bombarding you with "investment opportunities"), and all that planning can get quite complex. The wealth management becomes more of a chore than anything, like cleaning a house. Yes, rich people can and do clean their own houses, but if the house is very large, there are certainly people who can clean it better, faster, and more efficiently. Most importantly, wealthy people usually value their time and would rather spend it doing something other than managing money. Here the investment advisor plays a key role, to organize the finances of the wealthy, like a personal CFO. In the case of high-net-worth clients, I recommend they seek out a skilled professional, the fees are worth it. Because of the complexity of these situations, a good personal CFO will save you a lot of money and even more stress. They will also probably recommend a few unique winning investments to you as well.

Both of these scenarios acknowledge the value of a financial advisor. In the case of someone unable to make the decisions themselves, an advisor can play the caretaker. In the case of the wealth advisor dealing with a high net worth client, well let's be honest, if you are rich, you have better things to do than worry about the details of getting richer.

I'm not saying that there is absolutely no value in the services provided by the average financial planner. They simply must start adding <u>real</u> value if they hope to retain the next generation of investor. That value may not be in the form of performance, but at a minimum, it should be through quality information and education to enable the investor to stick to a solid plan. Many of my friends don't have a clue about what is being explained to them when they sit in front their financial planner/mutual fund salesperson; all they know is they are confused and unhappy about it. The new wave of investor is becoming more educated and better equipped to see through the thin veil of actively managed mutual funds.

DON'T WORRY IF YOU'RE NOT THE CLASS VALEDICTORIAN

Just remember, even though you may not be the best in math, chemistry, history, or English, these are subjects only studied in school. When you step out into the real word, few people will care about your grade on your last history final. They are going to care about what you can bring to their company, team, or project. There are unlimited subjects out there, and the most beautiful thing is that you get to choose which to pursue. The world is your oyster; you can choose to do whatever you want, so spend some time thinking about what you would be good at and go after it. It has been proven time and time again, that people excel at what they enjoy, and people get satisfaction from excelling in their job or business. It is that extra effort that really counts. Everyone worth their salt can give the basic minimum, but it's those that enjoy what they do who will consistently put in the extra effort. Those people are the winners; I say that everyone can be a winner, they just need to make sure they are playing the right game. If you want to find areas in which you excel, try visiting *strengthsfinder.com*.[27]

Being an avid lover of football, I will give you my first football analogy. Football is a fantastic game, and there's no doubt that there are some very skilled players. The largest factor between winning and losing in football, is positioning. If the players aren't in the right place at the correct time, no points will be scored. It's the same thing in life: as a player in the game of life, you have to figure out where you should be and where you will excel. There is no point in trying to be the quarterback when you are a natural kicker; the faster you discover your kicking skill, the faster you can develop it.

In football, there is always a coach, someone who has studied the game for years, who tells the players where to be and when. In life, you will be lucky if you have guidance from a parent or a mentor who can give you some great advice, but many people don't have that, so it will be up to you. Learn about yourself, know yourself, find out your strengths and weaknesses by trying many different things. That's the great thing about trying something new: even if you are terrible at it or hate it, at least you will learn something new about yourself. If you don't have a mentor, books and autobiographies can teach you a lot. Pick someone you think you will like, and find out what they have to teach you as you read about their life.

I have been a mentor for many students in the past. One thing I always tell my students is that, they need to figure out where their passion lies. They can't try to fit through a round hole if they are a square peg. You can completely change your chances of success by making sure you are in the right game. The faster you find the game that's right for you, the faster you will naturally develop your talents and begin to excel. If you don't know what your passion is, try everything and see what you like.

I believe this idea of academic success versus life success is the reason so many A+ students are employed by B and C students. The A students had focused so long on their competence in academia, that they often lost sight of the 'positioning' aspect of the game. Ask most B and C students, they can tell you how they knew from an early age that they would never be the top student in the class. This realization forces these students to find other ways to compete and other areas to excel.

I always had good grades, not great but good. I knew any job I got wasn't going to be as a result of my grades, but rather on what I had done with my life. Since my first job out of university (which lasted all of two months), I was never asked to submit a transcript. In my business endeavors, I've never been asked for my report card. In the grand scheme, grades truly don't matter that much; what matters is ability to apply knowledge and attitude to real life situations.

Business is a beautiful playing ground because one needs to be able to multi-task. Very rarely will a single skill or even a narrow set of skills get you to the top. You must be flexible and capable in a variety of areas. When you read about the successful business men and women in history, you will notice that it was almost never their competence in a school subject that led to their success. More often than not, it was their ability to manage people and understand a broad set of ideas.

Knowing this and understanding that there are many types of intelligence, I think it's fair to say that, we as a society have a very narrow view of intelligence. In fact, we really do define intelligence by a handful of benchmarks, like IQ tests and SAT scores. I believe the smartest people are those who can figure out where they excel and develop themselves in their own area of expertise. The most successful people are the ones who know themselves and use it to their advantage.

While there are many different kinds of intelligence and skill, there is a single constant that is easily identifiable: competence. It doesn't matter if you work at McDonald's or at McDonald Dettwiler, that character trait is transportable. Just like the kids with the marshmallow, it's going to persist no matter how complex the work, because after a while, once you are up the learning curve, difficulty is fairly relative.

 There is a great book available on Amazon, by Jamilla Diallo. It's called: *Ten Bad Habits We Learn in School*. It expands on many of the points I have mentioned here. Everyone should read this very short book; it is incredible in helping to get to know yourself, especially if you feel like one of those square pegs trying to fit through a round hole, like I was.

PREPARING FOR THE FUTURE

This is a special message for those who are reading this while trying to decide whether to attend university or pursue some other post secondary education. First, I would like to congratulate you on doing something to educate yourself on financial literacy; hats off to you, indeed. You, more than anyone, will be able to take advantage of all the advice in here and out there to improve you finances. Second, I can't stress enough the importance of a debt free graduation. I know it seems like a daunting task to be able to work your way through school, but after reading this book, I think you can see the value of graduating with money in your pocket, instead of thousands of dollars in debt. I encourage you to project your budget, and take a look at what these years will truly cost you. While I was in school, my military reservist paycheck and my stock trading profits, did much to help me through. I was also the deputy ombudsman for the university for one year, I interned with a wealth management company, and I started a financial literacy course. These activities/jobs didn't take away from the experience, but enhanced it. You may be concerned that you won't have enough time to work and study. I can tell you with complete certainty that it teaches you the very important skills of task prioritization and time optimization. It has been shown in multiple studies that having a part time job during school actually increases GPA. Your actions and studies become more efficient when you know you have responsibilities to attend to. What's more, the free time you do have is that much more rewarding. Push yourself hard in the short term, so you can be miles ahead of the start line when you graduate; that's always my philosophy.

If a student loan is inevitable, don't lose heart; there are many benefits for Canadian students applying for loans. If you are applying for a loan, you may also be eligible for a bursary or grant. Unlike a loan, these are contributions that are not expected to be repaid. The distribution of these gifts are on a "need" basis. If you are a student in need of assistance, bursaries, grants, and scholarships are your friend. Learn about them and how to access as many as possible; apply for everything, because you never know. I was lucky enough to receive thousands of dollars in 'free' money each year of university; I always tell people, that with that money I was able to pay for my second education, because it's the money I used to start investing!

I would also encourage you to use your university years to try new things and experiment with new ways of making money. My business partner and high school friend, Peter, used to buy old cars and fix them for resale. He made it through school with money in his pocket. I have other friends who worked as waitresses, bartenders, bouncers, and swim instructors. I know people who started small tech companies and designed software, and some who ran big parties and promoted events. There are so many cool things that you can do and capitalize on. Get out there, and seize the day!

THE IMPORTANCE OF ETHICS

It seems everywhere you turn these days, there is a scandal being uncovered; political and financial scandals seem to be people's favorite, because the effects of these types of scandals are so far-reaching. No one trusts anyone in the business world anymore, and who can blame people for not trusting institutions? I recently read an article focused on the least trusted industries: #1 Financial Services, #2 Banks, #3 Media, #4 Energy, #5 Pharmaceuticals. Does this surprise anyone? No. Why not? Because we have been conditioned to accept the fact that, those in a position of power are likely to abuse that power.

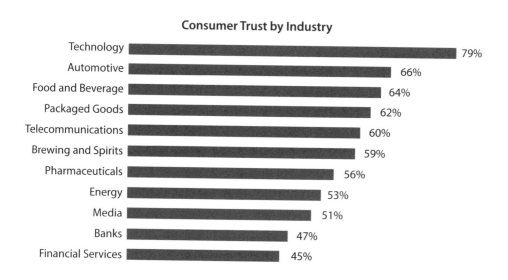

Consumer Trust by Industry

Technology	79%
Automotive	66%
Food and Beverage	64%
Packaged Goods	62%
Telecommunications	60%
Brewing and Spirits	59%
Pharmaceuticals	56%
Energy	53%
Media	51%
Banks	47%
Financial Services	45%

Data Source: Financialbrand.com

I write this so that you can plan for your future. When it comes to you and your decisions, consider the fact that there are people in the business community who have integrity; find those people and hang on to them. I saw an interesting *TED talk by Rachel Botsman,*[28] where she discussed reputation or trust, serving as currency. There is value in the idea, and as we move forward in the future, the abuses of power and trust in the past will cause people in the future to use "trustworthiness" as a larger part of their decision making process when deciding where to do business.

TALKING THE TALK HELPS YOU WALK THE WALK

I was always well aware that being born in Canada was the single most important event in my financial life. The advantages of winning the location lottery are phenomenal; I'm thankful every day for this blessing. I always knew that I wanted to give some of what I earned to those who had less. What I have found is that people don't talk about giving back very often. I believe that when you voice your opinion on an issue, it influences you to act in accordance with your comments. This is a very good thing, and I use it to keep myself in check.

The type of person you are before you are wealthy or financially free will remain the same once you are wealthy. Cash is just a catalyst to allow you to be more of what you already were. If you were already generous and loving, more money will allow you to be more so; the opposite is also true. I hope that knowing this ahead of time, will help to ensure the readers of this book always remain cognizant and vigilant about what money influences them to become. I hope you are able to set good habits at an early stage, and talk freely about these habits, as these comments will help keep one on the straight and narrow. Talk the talk, tell people your thoughts, ideas, hopes, and dreams about sharing your success and your wealth with those less fortunate. That way you will feel much fulfillment when you follow through, and it will be so much easier to do.

"You can easily judge the character of a man by how he treats those who can do nothing for him."- Johann Wolfgang von Goethe

SMILING YOUR WAY TO THE TOP

I must admit that it took far too long for me to recognize the power and importance of this subject. For the most part, we don't think too hard about how we interact with others. In my opinion, it is the single most important determinant of your success in almost everything you do. People will be much more likely to follow a leader who genuinely cares about their well being and shows it. I had heard this idea many times and disregarded the value in that advice. All that changed with a single book.

Dale Carnegie: *How to Win Friends and Influence People*, this book is written in a way that someone with my analytical style of thinking can see the quantifiable value in treating others like gold. As you progress in your journey and climb the ladder of success, you will be able to observe many types of people and how they interact with others. You will see great leaders and you may one day be a leader yourself. Being a great leader or even a great colleague doesn't always come naturally.

We interact with people everyday, and we spend far too little time studying how to maximize the value in those interactions. Some people have a natural talent for human interaction, but most of us really could use some work. What's more, it's actually a healthier way of living; I am a big believer that consistent positive thoughts and interactions can lead to a healthier body and mind. I encourage you to do some of your own research on how a positive outlook can improve your health.

If you find that you are lacking in your ability to get into a good mood and stay there, the first thing you should do is take a look at the people with whom you spend most of your time. It is said that the 5 people you spend the most time with, influence you the most; their traits tend to rub off on you and yours on them. It is also said that these important people will have a strong influence on not only the quality of your mood, but your health and wealth also. The easiest way to change yourself is to change your surroundings and your friends.

Watch your thoughts, for they become words.
Watch your words, for they become actions.
Watch your actions, for they become habits.
Watch your habits, for they become character.
Watch your character, for it becomes your destiny."
- Lao Tzu

BE A FORWARD THINKER

Always remember to keep the next generation in mind. They will have to inherit your successes and your failures; you do not want to force them to spend their lives paying for your mistakes. Too often we act with such short-sightedness, when we could have done so much better by simply demanding smarter solutions.

Our dependency on oil and pharmaceuticals are two prime examples of this. If we took our focus off profits and put it on to our children, do you think we would be facing extreme environmental and health crises? I believe that all we have to do sometimes, is demand a better solution and not settle because we have found something that's "good enough for now."

BEWARE THE WORSHIP OF MONEY

I will leave you with a word of caution. I'm aware that the main focus of this book is wealth. However, the intention of this book is not to help you to be rich for richness sake. It's to help you towards financial freedom for the benefit of yourself, your family, and the world. Everyone should want to leave this world better than they found it for the next generation. One of the easiest ways to distract yourself from this idea is to focus only on personal gain and personal wealth alone. It is my hope that you resist the temptation to focus solely on the generation of personal wealth, and visualize your success as a means to the improve the world. Money has a way of hypnotizing people and helping them to forget the reason they wanted the money in the first place. Do not fall for that fallacy; do not lose the focus, intentions, and the good habits you establish early on.

MOTIVATION AND SUCCESS

Life will give you what you expect: so expect a lot. I'd like to leave you with some inspirational material, all of which I found useful. If you feel your motivation is lacking, listen to Arnold Schwarzenegger's, *Motivation Speech*[29] or Eric Thomas, The Hip Hop Philosopher's, *Success....How Bad Do You Want It?*[30] Will Smith also provides some inspirational material in his interview, *Will Smith Shares His Secret Of Success.*[31]

Happy investing. Good Luck!

ABOUT THE AUTHOR

Mark Ameerali grew up in the Fraser Valley. He attended private schools in Surrey, BC, for both elementary and high school. He was always interested in studying how the money world worked. By his 20's, he knew he wanted to learn how to make money work for him, instead of the other way around. Upon entering university, he began his formal financial education in 2002, with the Canadian Securities Course. He attended UBC's Sauder School of Business, graduating with a specialization in finance.

While at UBC, he gained experience in retail banking and wealth management through internships at HSBC and RBCDS. Upon graduation, Mark began his career in commercial banking and progressed to pension fund management after a short time, which marked the beginning of his postgraduate education.

Mark left his position with a Vancouver investment counsel and his home, to study for the prestigious Chartered Financial Analyst program (CFA), in South Korea. He completed the program in 2010. To help finance his various adventures, Mark designed a course in personal finance and investments. In each city he lived, he offered his course, and the course has been condensed into the book you are reading.

Upon his return to Canada in 2011, Mark spent time looking for ways to align his work life with his goal of both achieving his financial freedom and helping others to achieve theirs. This led him to start the real estate consulting company Maplequity, with a partner and friend, Peter Latta. The freedom afforded to him through business ownership allowed him the time to write this book. In addition to founding Maplequity, Mark worked with a Canadian real estate education company, creating a mutual fund trust for U.S. cross border investment.

Currently, Mark is working with one of Canada's leading exempt market dealers (EMDs), helping Canadians access direct investments in private companies. He also continues to run Maplequity while teaching financial literacy in Kelowna. Mark has dedicated his life to increasing the financial literacy of Canadians, in the hope that they can give of themselves to others in the ways they desire.

149

Website References

All web links and bonus material can be found on my website:

www.mymoneysense.ca

CHAPTER 1

1. Government of Canada: Financial Consumer Agency Education Section
2. Income Tax Calculator
3. TurboTax
4. Taxbot
5. David M. Voth
6. Canada Revenue Agency

CHAPTER 2

7. Don't Eat The Marshmallow
8. TED.com
9. Equifax Canada
10. Transunion Canada
11. Mint
12. The Canadian Mortgage Housing Corporation
13. Mortgage Calculator

CHAPTER 3

14. Money Chimp

CHAPTER 4

15. Investopedia

CHAPTER 5

16. Mission Improbable by Ken French
17. Ontario Securities Commission
18. Ontario Securities Commission's Interactive Chart
19. Online Retirement Savings Calculator

CHAPTER 7

20. Canadian Couch Potato

CHAPTER 8

21. Google: Exempt Market Dealers (your city)

CHAPTER 11

22. Fidelity's Investment Planning Tool
23. Index Funds Website- IFA.com
24. Sequence of Portfolios
25. Ontario Government
26. Google: Exempt Market Dealers (your city)

CHAPTER 12

27. Strengthsfinder.com
28. Ted Talk By Rachel Botsman
29. Arnold Schwarzenegger's Motivation Speech
30. Eric Thomas, The Hip Hop Philosopher- Success... How Bad Do You Want It?
31.Will Smith Shares His Secret of Success

Book References

Bogle, John C. (2007). *The Little Book Of Common Sense Investing. The Only Way to Guarantee Your Fair Share of Stock Market Returns.* United States: *Wiley.*

Cardy, Sandy, Fitzgerald, Mike (2003). *The Cottage, the Spider Brooch, and the Second Wife: How to Overcome the Challenges of Estate Planning.* Ontario, Canada: ECW Press.

Carnegie, Dale (1990). *How To Win Friends And Influence People.* United States: Pocket Books.

Chilton, David (1998). *The Wealthy Barber: Everyone's Commonsense Guide to Becoming Financially Independent (3rd edition).* United States: Crown Business.

Chilton, David (2011). *The Wealthy Barber Returns.* Ontario, Canada: Financial Awareness Corporation.

Covey, Stephen R. (1989). *7 Habits of Highly Effective People.* New York: Free Press.

Diallo, Jamila (2011). *Ten Bad Habits We Learn In School.* United States: Smashwords Inc.

Greenblatt, Joel (2011). *The Big Secret for the Small Investor: A New Route to Long-Term Investment Success.* United States: Crown Business.

Hebner, Mark T. (2005). *Index Funds: The 12-Step Recovery Program for Active Investors.* United States: IFA Publishing Inc.

Kiyosaki, Robert (2011). *Rich Dad Poor Dad: What the Rich Teach Their Kids About Money, That the Poor and Middle Class Do Not!* United States: Plata Publishing.

Kiyosaki, Robert (2011). *Rich Dad's Cashflow Quadrant: Guide to Financial*

Freedom. United States: Plata Publishing.

Kiyosaki, Robert (2003). *Rich Dad's Guide to Investing: What the Rich Invest In, That the Poor and Middle Class Do Not!* United States: Warner books.

Kiyosaki, Robert (2011). *Unfair Advantage: The Power Of Financial Education.* United States: Plata Publishing.

Matthews, Keith (2008). *The Empowered Investor. A Guide To Building Better Portfolios.* Ontario, Canada: Book Coach Press.

Moxley, Richard (2012). *What The Average Joe Needs To Know: The Nine Rules Of Credit.* Canada

Murray, Nick (1999). *Simple Wealth, Inevitable Wealth: How You and Your Financial Advisor Can Grow Your Fortune in Stock Mutual Funds.* United States: The Nick Murray Company Inc.

Peckford, Scott, W. *How To Rob Your Bank. Perfectly Legal, Insider Tips to Save Money on Your Mortgage.* Canada: Franklin Bradford Press.

Tyson, Eric, MBA, Martin, Tony (2007). *Personal Finance For Canadians For Dummies* (4th Edition). United States: For Dummies.

Voth, David, M. (2006). *The 10 Secrets Revenue Canada Doesn't Want You to Know* (Revised and Expanded Edition). Canada: Centax Books and Distribution.

Glossary

ACCREDITED INVESTORS

A term used by the Securities Commission to refer to investors who are financially sophisticated and have a reduced need for the protection provided by certain government filings. Accredited investors include affluent or high net worth individuals, banks, insurance companies, employee benefit plans, and trusts.

Common requirements for accredited investors include:

$1 million in financial assets
$5 million in net total assets (including real estate)
$200,000 in pre-tax annual income for the last two years
$300,000 in pre-tax annual income for the last two years with a spouse.

AD VALOREM FEE

A fee based on the value of the account on which it is levied.

ANALYSIS PARALYSIS

The overthinking of a decision to the point where no decision can be made.

BANKRUPT

A legal proceeding involving a person or business that is unable to repay outstanding debts. Upon the successful completion of bankruptcy proceedings, the debtor is relieved of the debt obligations incurred prior to filing for bankruptcy.

BOARD LOT

A standardized number of shares defined by a stock exchange as a trading unit. In most cases, this means 100 shares. The purpose of a board lot is to avoid "odd lots" and to facilitate easier trading. It's more difficult for a broker to find a buyer for, say, 17 shares, than if everybody agrees to trade in 100 share lots. The thinking is that standardization increases liquidity thus lowering spreads and making the market more efficient for everybody.

BONA FIDE

In good faith; without deception or fraud; authentic; true.

BOOK VALUE

The value at which an asset is carried on a balance sheet. To calculate, take the cost of an asset minus the accumulated depreciation. By being compared to the company's market value, the book value can indicate whether a stock is under or overpriced.

CARRIED INTEREST

A share of any profits that the general partners of private equity and hedge funds receive as compensation, despite not contributing any initial funds. This method of compensation seeks to motivate the general partner (fund manager) to work toward improving the fund's performance.

CONSUMER PRICE INDEX

A measure that examines the weighted average of prices of a basket of consumer goods and services, such as transportation, food, and medical care. The CPI is calculated by taking price changes for each item in the predetermined basket of goods and averaging them; the goods are weighted according to their importance. Changes in CPI are used to assess price changes associated with the cost of living.

CONTINUOUS DISCLOSURE

Companies that are reporting issuers on the public market must regularly make certain information about their activities and financial status available to the public. Many of these requirements are set out in the following rules:

- *National Instrument 51-102 Continuous Disclosure Obligations* sets out the obligations for ongoing filing and disclosure requirements.
- *National Instrument 52-107 Acceptable Accounting Principles, Auditing Standards and Reporting Currency* sets out the accounting principles and auditing standards that apply to financial statements filed.
- *National Instrument 52-109 Certification of Disclosure in Issuers' Annual and Interim Filings* sets out certification requirements for reporting issuers other than investment funds.
- *National Instrument 71-102 Continuous Disclosure and Other Exemptions Relating to Foreign Issuers* outlines exemptions for certain foreign issuers from most continuous disclosure requirements and certain other requirements.

CORRELATION

In the world of finance, this is a statistical measure of how two securities move in relation to each other. Correlations are used in advanced portfolio management.

DIVIDEND DISCOUNT MODEL

A procedure for valuing the price of a stock by using predicted dividends and discounting them back to present value. The idea is that if the value obtained from the DDM is higher than what the shares are currently trading at, then the stock is undervalued.

EFFICIENT MARKET HYPOTHESIS

An investment theory that states it is impossible to "beat the market", because stock market efficiency causes existing share prices to always incorporate and reflect all relevant information. According to the EMH, stocks always trade at their fair value on stock exchanges, making it impossible for investors to either purchase undervalued stocks or sell stocks for inflated prices. As such, it should be impossible to outperform the overall market through expert stock selection or market timing, and that the only way an investor can possibly obtain higher returns is by purchasing riskier investments.

ELIGIBLE INVESTORS

An individual, who either alone or with a spouse owns net assets (including real estate) exceeding $400,000. Or an individual whose net income before taxes exceeded $75,000, or together with a spouse exceed $125,000 in the two previous years, and reasonably expects to exceed that level in the current year. Or a person registered, or previously registered under the securities legislation of a jurisdiction of Canada as an adviser or dealer, other than a limited dealer registered under the Securities Act (Ontario) or the Securities Act (Newfoundland and Labrador).

ENDOWMENT

A financial asset donation made to a non-profit group or institution in the form of investment funds or other property that has a stated purpose at the bequest of the donor. Most endowments are designed to keep the principal amount intact while using the investment income from dividends for charitable efforts.

EXCHANGE-TRADED FUND (ETF)

A security that tracks an index, a commodity or a basket of assets like an index fund, but trades like a stock on an exchange. ETFs experience price changes throughout the day as they are bought and sold.

EXEMPT MARKET DEALER

An entity registered to distribute exempt/private market securities. Exempt market dealers are registered with and regulated by provincial regulatory bodies.

EXEMPT MARKET SECURITIES

Exempt market securities are securities issued in Canada that fall under National Instrument 45-106. They are exempt from prospectus requirements, and hence require less disclosure than a prospectus offering. To sell a security in the exempt market, an issuer must ensure that the investor qualifies under a specific exemption contained in the Instrument.

HIGH WATERMARK

The highest peak in value that an investment fund/account has reached. This term is often used in the context of fund manager compensation, which is performance based.

HURDLE RATE

The minimum rate of return on a project or investment by a manager or investor. In order to compensate for risk, the riskier the project, the higher the hurdle rate. In the hedge fund world, hurdle rate refers to the rate of return that the fund manager must beat before collecting incentive fees.

INVESTMENT POLICY STATEMENT

A document drafted between a portfolio manager and a client that outlines general rules for the manager. This statement provides the general investment goals and objectives of a client and describes the strategies that the manager should employ to meet these objectives. Specific information on matters such as asset allocation, risk tolerance, and liquidity requirements would also be included in an IPS.

LEVERAGE

The use of various financial instruments or borrowed capital, such as margin, to increase the potential return of an investment.

ALSO: The amount of debt used to finance a firm's assets. A firm with significantly more debt than equity is considered to be highly leveraged. Leverage is most commonly used in real estate transactions through the use of mortgages to purchase a home.

LEVERAGED BUYOUTS

The acquisition of another company using a significant amount of borrowed money (bonds or loans) to meet the cost of acquisition. Often, the assets of the company being acquired are used as collateral for the loans in addition to the assets of the acquiring company. The purpose of leveraged buyouts is to allow companies to make large acquisitions without having to commit a lot of capital.

LIQUIDITY

The ability to convert an asset to cash quickly. Also known as "marketability". The degree to which an asset or security can be bought or sold in the market without affecting the asset's price. Liquidity is characterized by a high level of trading activity. Assets that can be easily bought or sold are known as liquid assets.

LOCKUP PERIOD

The window of time in which investors of a hedge fund or other closely-held investment vehicle are not allowed to redeem or sell shares. The lock-up period helps portfolio managers avoid liquidity problems while capital is put to work in sometimes illiquid investments.

MARGIN

Borrowed money that is used to purchase securities. This practice is referred to as "buying on margin".

NOMINAL RETURN

The amount of money generated by an investment before expenses such as taxes, investment fees, and inflation are factored in. For example, detailed data on a mutual fund might show a fund's nominal rate of return as 10%, but also show its return after taxes on distributions and sale of fund shares is only 7%. Investors should look beyond an investment's nominal rate of return to get a true idea of what their investment will earn.

ODD LOT

An order amount for a security that is less than the normal unit of trading for that particular asset. Odd lots are considered to be anything less than the standard 100 shares for stocks. Trading commissions for odd lots are generally higher on a percentage basis than those for standard lots, since most brokerage firms have a fixed minimum commission level for undertaking such transactions.

OFFERING MEMORANDUM

A legal document stating the objectives, risks, and terms of investment involved with a private placement. This includes items such as the financial statements, management biographies, detailed description of the business, etc. An offering memorandum serves to provide buyers with information on the offering and to protect the sellers from the liability associated with selling unregistered securities.

OPPORTUNITY COST

The cost of the next best option that is forgone in lieu of the chosen option. It is the sacrifice related to the seond best choice or investment.

OVERSIGHT

The supervision of a regulatory body of the information provided and the processes of a market.

PASSIVE INCOME

Earnings an individual derives from a rental property, limited partnership, or other enterprise in which he or she is not actively involved.

PENSION FUND

A fund established by an employer to facilitate and organize the investment of employees' retirement funds contributed by the employer and employees. The pension fund is a common asset pool meant to generate stable growth over the long term, and provide pensions for employees when they reach the end of their working years and commence retirement.

PRIMARY MARKET

The primary markets are where investors can get first crack at a new security issuance. The issuing company or group receives cash proceeds from the sale, which is then used to fund operations or expand the business. Primary markets are facilitated by underwriting groups, which consist of investment banks that will set a beginning price range for a given security and then oversee its sale directly to investors.

PROSPECTUS

A formal legal document, which is required by and filed with the Securities and Exchange Commission, that provides details about an investment offering for sale to the public. A prospectus should contain the facts that an investor needs to make an informed investment decision.

RETURN ON INVESTMENT (ROI)

A performance measure used to evaluate the efficiency of an investment or to compare the efficiency of a number of different investments. To calculate ROI, the benefit (return) of an investment is divided by the cost of the investment; the result is expressed as a percentage or a ratio.

SECONDARY MARKET

A market where investors purchase securities or assets from other investors, rather than from issuing companies themselves. The national exchanges, Toronto Stock Exchange, New York Stock Exchange, and the NASDAQ, are secondary markets.

SECTOR

An industry or market sharing common characteristics. Investors use sectors to place stocks and other investments into categories like technology, health care, energy, utilities, and telecommunications. Each sector has unique characteristics and a different risk profile.

SECURITY MARKET LINE

A line that graphs the systematic or market risk versus return of the whole market at a certain time and shows all risky marketable securities.

SHORT SELL

The selling of a security that the seller does not own, or any sale that is completed by the delivery of a security borrowed by the seller. Short sellers assume that they will be able to buy the stock at a lower amount than the price at which they sold short. Short sellers make money if the stock goes down in price. This is an advanced trading strategy with many unique risks and pitfalls. Novice investors are advised to avoid short sales.

SMALL CAP STOCKS

Refers to stocks with a relatively small market capitalization. The definition of small cap can vary among brokerages, but generally it is a company with a market capitalization of between $300 million and $2 billion.

SOLE PROPRIETOR

The sole proprietor is an unincorporated business with one owner who pays personal income tax on profits from the business. With little government regulation, they are the simplest business to set up or take apart, making them popular among individual self contractors or business owners.

VARIABLE

Liable to vary or change.

Glossary terms courtesty of Investopedia

NOTES:

_____

_____

_____

_____

_____

_____

_____

_____

_____

_____

_____

_____

_____

_____

_____

_____

_____

_____

_____

_____

_____

_____

_____

_____

_____

_____

_____

_____

NOTES:

NOTES:

NOTES:

NOTES:

NOTES:

NOTES:

NOTES:

NOTES: